TODAY'

Book 3 – The Fivefold Office ...

COLETTE TOACH

AMI BOOKSHOP

www.ami-bookshop.com

Today's Pastor
Book 3 – The Fivefold Office Series

ISBN-10: 1626640378
ISBN-13: 978-1-62664-037-5

1st Printing July 2016

Published by **Apostolic Movement International, LLC**
E-mail Address: admin@ami-bookshop.com
Web Address: www.ami-bookshop.com

Contents

Chapter 01 – The Two-fold Pastoral Function 8

The Two-fold Pastoral Function 9

The New Testament Pastor 10

Two-fold Function: Elder and Overseer 12

Primary Pastoral Function: Minister 15

Second Pastoral Function: Administrator 16

Pastoral Training – Transition From Elder to Shepherd 19

Maturing the Church 21

Chapter 02 – Understanding the Position of Overseer 26

Delegation of Authority 26

Fivefold Ministry Overseers 33

Apostolic Authority Passed Down 34

Chapter 03 – The Pattern for the Pastor 36

Being the Shepherd 37

Appointment + Anointed = Pastor 38

The Pastor in the Local Church 40

Spot the Pastor 41

Becoming a Leader of Thousands 42

The Early Church Pastoral Example 47

Who is Your Pastor? 52

Chapter 04 – Identifying Today's Pastor 56

A Place to Belong...58

Making the Church a Place to Belong......................60

The Pastoral Calling 63

The Old Testament Pastor.......................................67

Leadership Set in Place..70

Responsibilities of the Priests 72

Chapter 05 – The Transition to Shepherd 78

The New Testament 80

New Testament Comparison....................................83

The Birth of Another Nation 84

Chapter 06 – Signs of Today's Pastor 92

1. Feels Called to a Community (Stays at Home).....93

2. Likes Practical Teaching (Breaks Down Doctrine into Practical Teaching) 96

4. Gets Personal (Corrects and Encourages) 98

5. Core Desire: To help others...............................104

6. Takes Care of the Church! (Takes Care of the Temple) 105

7. Does Not "Let Go" of People Easily 108

8. Protective Over the Flock 109

9. The "Jack-of-all-Trades" Anointing...................112

10. Ministry to the Church 114

The Ruler that Serves 115

Chapter 07 – The Pastor's Purpose 120

Mass Influx of New Believers 120

Enter: Today's Pastors..121

The Shepherd Who Succeeds...............................123

Preparing the Soil for Revival 132

Gather the Flock 133

Perfection is Overrated 139

Your Training Starts Here – The Secret 140

About the Author 142

Recommendations by the Author 144

The Fivefold Offices for Today...............................144

Today's Evangelist 145

The Minister's Handbook 145

How to Get People to Follow You 146

How to Hear the Voice of God (Study Group Kit)..146

Fivefold Ministry School 147

Contact Information 148

THE TWO-FOLD PASTORAL FUNCTION

Chapter 01 – The Two-fold Pastoral Function

I am going to take you on a journey. One that will have some twists and turns and a few sudden changes of topic. By the time we are done though, you will know, what a pastor is, how he is called, and what he is meant to be doing in the Church!

I will push you directly into the deep end with some teaching on the two-fold function of the pastor, before giving you some clear signs of what the ministry of the pastor looks like.

For those who have this nagging feeling that God is indeed calling them to fulfill this function in the Church, I have some guidelines of what your purpose of a pastor should be, as it relates to this apostolic move upon us.

There are some things I need you to keep in mind as you continue to read. This is a book about Today's Pastor. We have seen this position change so many times through the years and as God's people go through various phases of maturity, so also does the position need to become more, and do more than ever before!

Our status quo picture of a pastor behind the pulpit every day is fast shifting and now we see pastors who live stream meetings, establish group homes, counsel one on one and participate in ministry centers, using a variety of ministry skills.

The Church is changing. Rather I should say, the Church is conforming to the pattern that God has established for it. Along with the revelation of the fivefold ministry, comes a deeper understanding of the role of the pastor in this blueprint, the place the pastor fills, and how this works beautifully with the rest of the fivefold ministry.

So no – this is not a book about going to bible college and being given a pastorate and parish. This is about Today's Pastor and what exactly that means to you right now.

The Two-fold Pastoral Function

1 Peter 5:1-4

> *The elders who are among you I exhort, I who am a fellow elder and a witness of the sufferings of Christ, and also a partaker of the glory that will be revealed:*
> *2 Shepherd the flock of God which is among you, serving as overseers, not by compulsion but willingly, not for dishonest gain but eagerly;*
> *3 nor as being lords over those entrusted to you, but being examples to the flock;*
> *4 and when the Chief Shepherd appears, you will receive the crown of glory that does not fade away.*

I am going to kick start this teaching with a clear understanding of the office of the pastor. I think everyone will agree with me about the ministry function of the pastor. It is not a stretch to see the pastor as a shepherd or to imagine his heart for the sheep.

However, what I want to bring to your attention in this scripture that is so profound is this: The function of the pastor is two-fold.

This is where things get tricky! You get two imbalances in the Church. You get the pastor that is all about position and leadership and then you get the pastor that is all about feeding the sheep. So, imagine my surprise when the Lord showed me clearly, though this passage, that today's pastor needs to be both!

In this short passage, we see how Peter speaks of the pastoral ministry using two different words.

Paul calls them shepherds and elders. The pastoral function is a very unique ministry. By the end of the next few chapters, you are going to know what a pastor looks like, and what a pastor should be doing in both the local and universal Church.

The first thing that I want to bring to your mind is that the pastor has two jobs. This is what has brought confusion in the body of Christ.

The New Testament Pastor

We have the camp where we have one pastor who stands up in a megachurch and he is in control of everything. Then we have another camp where we have a prophet saying, "Forget this 'pastor' nonsense. Let us throw the pastor off his pedestal and bring in the fivefold ministry. Who needs the pastor anyway?"

To complicate matters, when you look in the New Testament at the word "pastor" or "pastors," you will find that it is only listed once – twice if you include Acts 20:28 where the word "Shepherd" is mentioned. Only one time is it listed as pastor, and the other as pastors. It seems strange at first.

This is one of the fivefold ministry and it is hardly even mentioned. Now before you jump to conclusions, realize that the pastor is most certainly mentioned. Throughout the Old Testament, the word elders, overseers, bishops and shepherds are mentioned many times. Used interchangeably, these words refer to the same ministry type.

It can get a little confusing because we have the concept of an overseer -someone who is in charge and holds a position. Then we have this concept of the ministry orientation of the guy who has the pastor's heart and feeds God's flock.

Then, Peter jumps in as an apostle and says, "I am also an elder like you guys." (1Peter 5:1) What is going on here? What is a pastor? What is an elder? What is an overseer? What is a bishop? They are all one and the same thing, but they are encased in two separate functions.

One is a function that is given by man and the other is a function that is given by God.

I want you to understand the difference between an administrative and ministry appointment in the body of Christ.

When we begin to look through the Word of God with these eyes, then the New Testament begins to explode with new revelation. As I came to study the pastor, I realized why the Apostles kept using the words elder and overseer, and just threw in pastor in a couple places.

Two-fold Function: Elder and Overseer

The Word says that the elders laid hands on Paul and Barnabas and committed them to the work. (Acts 13:1-2) So, pastors are now imparting and appointing apostles to the work? Then, it gets more confusing because it says that there were some amongst them that were pastors, and some teachers, and so on.

What is going on? It is because the pastoral ministry is like the evangelistic ministry in this one regard - it is one of the most basic functions of ministry. I hear people saying all the time, "The Lord has called me to be a prophet, not a pastor. God has called me to be an apostle, not a pastor."

If you are called to ministry in any form, then you are called to pastor God's people. Why? It is because you are called to feed and mature the flock. You may be an elder and even have other fivefold ministries.

Even when Paul speaks to Timothy, he says that elders must be apt to teach, they need to be pastor-teachers, they need to be able to take care of God's flock. Are you seeing these two functions? One is administrative and the other is spiritual.

Let us not confuse the two. When we look at the early church, we see Antioch springing up and we see Jerusalem experiencing a big move taking place in Samaria. These churches consisted of new converts, yet out of those, elders were put in place.

Appointed Position

We are talking about people that just started getting to know the Lord. They were not even in the Lord for years and spiritually sensitive enough to say, "I see upon him the pastoral ministry, so let us make him a pastor."

No. Elder simply means somebody that is mature and someone that people look up to. It was so obvious to Paul who the elders were. You can just see it if you go to a group of a bunch of believers. It is clear who the leaders are.

All Peter and Paul needed to do was look and see that obviously "this guy" is a leader and "that one" is a leader. Then, they laid hands on them and appointed them to the position of overseer and elder.

Did that suddenly make them pastors overnight? Does that mean that they could do the ministry of a pastor overnight? No. That is something that they had to grow into. However, they had to start somewhere.

Can you see that we need both functions in the body of Christ? Unfortunately, there have been two different extremes. On one extreme, you have just the overseer with no pastor's heart whatsoever. He has not learned to function properly as a pastor and feed the flock. He just fills the position.

Then, you have those with a true pastor's heart. They want to reach out to people, but they are not in a position to do any of that feeding. We need to bring the two together.

Ministry Function

When I first started training the prophets, as I rose up, the Lord said to me, "Colette, you need to start pastoring the prophets." I thought, "Lord, are you out of your mind? Me - a pastor?"

Maybe, you think that I am nice now, but you did not know me back in those days. I saw things as black and white, yes and no, up and down... there was no in-between. People trembled and feared me because I was this "big prophet" that just said it the way it was.

Then, the Lord said, "Be a pastor." I thought, "Lord, you have got the wrong person for the job." However, He told me that I need to pastor His prophets because they needed more than just prophetic office - they needed to be fed and ministered to.

I discovered, as a prophet in office, that I had to be a pastor, and I daresay that whether you are a prophet, apostle, or a teacher, if you have this element missing in your ministry, then you have one big lack.

Primary Pastoral Function: Minister

Let us consider the function of the pastor. He is the shepherd. He leads the sheep to still waters. He is the one that gives them the Word of God, encourages them to keep going. He is there when no one else is, and he gives counsel and advice for every part of life.

If you look at it as a household family, he is like the mom. I refer often to the pastor as one who mothers the church. He is the one that you go to when you fall and hurt your knee. He gives you counsel and teaches you to make it better.

A Spiritual Mother

I am sure that all of you have been in a ministry at some time or another where you did meet someone with a pastor's heart. You met someone who cared enough to get involved.

Unfortunately, we have separated it so much. You say, "You are a pastor. I am a prophet, evangelist, apostle, and so on." You are sitting there saying, "Let the pastors do their job. I am the teacher. I will do my job."

No. We need to minister to the Church universal in any way that God needs us to do it.

I feel such a challenge in my spirit, especially for those who are prophetic and have hidden away from this so much because they have seen the wrong picture from the Church. You are pushing away so much from this "pastor idea" because you are only seeing the overseer part.

You are not seeing that the prophetic ministry is both. It is being an overseer and having a ministry to heal the wounds of God's people. What we need to do is bring it together. Otherwise, we are never going to rise up and bring change to the Church.

Second Pastoral Function: Administrator

So, what is an elder and overseer? Firstly, it is one that is appointed by man. Acts 14:23 says,

> *So when they had appointed elders in every church, and prayed with fasting, they commended them to the Lord in whom they had believed.*

Titus 1:5 says,

> *For this reason I left you in Crete, that you should set in order the things that are lacking, and appoint elders in every city as I commanded you*

Wow. Again and again, we see the word "elders," but it did not start or originate in the New Testament. Exodus 18:25 says,

> *And Moses chose able men out of all Israel, and made them heads over the people: rulers of thousands, rulers of hundreds, rulers of fifties, and rulers of tens.*

There were seventy people of that group that were pulled out specifically, and the Lord said, "Bring those elders to me, Moses, and I will take that anointing that is upon you and I will place that anointing upon them."

Man Chose the Elders

Who chose the seventy? Moses did. It says right there that Moses chose able men. He looked around to see who was capable and who the obvious elders were, and then he pulled them out.

Then, out of those, they chose seventy leaders. When they brought those seventy leaders before the Lord, the Scriptures say that the Lord took the anointing that was on Moses and put it on them.

The Lord anointed them so that they could then go out. Two guys did not show up for the meeting. They were still in the camp. Then, they got a report that said those guys were prophesying in the camp.

That is the difference. On one hand, Moses appointed them and delegated to them his natural authority. He told them that he had been counseling and ministering, and he was getting to a point where he could not reach the masses anymore.

Jethro gave Moses a heads up and told him that he was going to kill himself doing all the work alone. You see, Moses was doing the megachurch thing. He was sitting there, morning to night, having people come with all their problems until he was finished.

Jethro told him that there must be a better way. He told Moses to appoint some leaders, spread the people out, and to reproduce himself. That is what Moses did. He got leaders of fifty, hundreds, and thousands.

Delegated Then Anointed

Out of those leaders, seventy really stood out and those were the ones that he brought before the Lord. Then, in addition to the delegated authority from Moses, they were anointed by God.

Let us not confuse the role of the pastor and be so quick to push him off of his pedestal because there is such a thing as a function of an overseer. It comes with delegated authority, and it is a position of leadership given due to spiritual maturity.

It is somebody that has been along the way and been through some leadership training and knows a little bit about life. That is why the elders and overseers in the New Testament had such a variety of callings.

A Variety of Leadership Functions

They were pastors. They were elders and shepherds. Yet, most of them did not stay there. Some of them rose up to be prophets, some teachers, and even Peter rose up to be an apostle.

However, every last one of them functioned as pastors as well. Therefore, when you are talking about those rising up in pastoral ministry, realize that it is a two-fold function in the church.

> **The call to pastor is an administrative position given by man and a ministry anointing given by God.**

When you look at the previous sections in the book, you will see how I taught you about the *ministry* of the pastor. To counsel, feed the sheep, and to flow in the anointing. I was teaching you to have a shepherd's heart, to be able to reach in, heal, and lead people in the right direction.

Pastoral Training – Transition From Elder to Shepherd

To function in this way takes ministry training. There is no man in this world that can get it from another man. I do not care how many years you study at bible college or how many years you read those books.

You cannot read up, study or "work up" the anointing. All you can do is perhaps become a good elder and overseer. However, until you have the ministry function as well, you do not have the completion of the pastor. You need both to fulfill the pastoral function in the Church.

Unfortunately, we see one or the other. We have all these seminaries where people are studying, and colleges where people think that if they earn their degree, then they will be given authority by man to preach in a church.

Elder vs. Pastor

Yes, you can do that and that makes you an elder, but are you a pastor? What about the other element? All you have is an appointment by man. So, does that mean that we should not respect them? No.

The authority has been delegated to them by the apostle. Yet, how effective are they going to be? They are not going to be effective at all. We have to bring the two together. However, we cannot throw out the baby with the bathwater either.

We need leaders in the body of Christ, and if God is calling you to rise up as a leader in the Church, then he is calling you to be a pastor. This is your foremost responsibility to the Church of God.

I did not push out my babies and hand them to my husband, Craig, and say, "Send them to college." No. There is a lot of stuff that happens in between there.

There is diaper changing, nose wiping, and getting up in the middle of the night.

There is a process to grow up a child. It is the same in the body of Christ. We keep wanting to skip to the leadership and the good stuff, but what about raising up the body of Christ to maturity?

Maturing the Church

Is that not what the pastor is meant to be doing? Is he not supposed to be taking the babies that the evangelist has brought in and grow them up? Now, they need two things to grow up.

They need someone to be in charge, and they need someone to feed them. It is easy. When I become a mother, I am put in charge. I am the boss in the house. Do not mess with my kitchen or my kids.

I am the boss, and my children need to learn and respect that authority. Yet, that is not my only function. My function is also to be there to meet their needs. Again, there are two functions. There is a function of authority and a function of ministry.

Now, we spoke about the evangelist and how he came and got the sheep on fire. We are producing lambs and we have new converts. Everyone is fired up and ready to go.

Now what? That is where the pastor comes in because we cannot leave them there.

Raising the Children of God

I cannot bear these evangelists that go out, evangelize, and just get people saved all over the place. They say, "I led somebody to the Lord today." Then, I think, "And…?" It is like getting pregnant, having babies, and then leaving them on the sidewalk and walking away.

These people are so excited to tell you about how many people they got saved. They say, "Well, I had two hundred babies this year." I am thinking, "Where are they?" They are scattered all over the place.

We would not do that in the natural, so why are we doing this to God's people?

When a sheep has a lamb, it takes care of the lamb. The shepherd does not say, "Good job. Now, let us do away with the lamb." No. He takes the lamb and nurtures it. He brings it to a place of maturity, so that it can become a sheep and produce more lambs.

We need to bring the body of Christ to maturity. We need to take the lambs that God has given us and follow through with them.

The evangelists have gone ahead, prepared the way, and gotten people on fire. Now, what do they do with that fire? How do they apply that fire to their lives and problems? How do they apply all that they are learning to the reality of life?

Functions in all Ministry Gifts

That is what the pastor teaches them. This is why the pastoral ministry functions in all nine gifts of the Spirit. Do you know why? It is because he is a bit like Mom. Mom is the doctor, nurse, and a little bit of everything.

She has to take care of all these different needs. You are a jack-of-all-trades and a master of none because you need to take the fire that people have, and teach them how to use it.

What is the use of just being fired up? When you make a fire in the natural it is to cook something, produce something, keep you warm – it always has a specific purpose. You do not just make a fire and walk away. What a waste of wood.

The evangelist may make the fire, but it is up to the pastor to come and say, "Let us utilize the power of this fire. Let us see what we can build. Let us make something or do something with this fire so that it matures."

Develops the Potential in Others

When you first start a fire, you have all these flames that shoot up, but then after a while the coals begin to glow. Then, that big fire starts to die down and it is those glowing coals that actually have the potential.

Those are what you use to cook your meat with. Nobody sticks their meat or marshmallows on an open flame (unless you are me) because otherwise it burns. You wait until the coals are hot and red and then you have something to work with.

That is when you use the heat. That is the job of the pastor. The evangelist gets in there and he gets a good fire started and it is good and burning. Then, he goes and starts another fire and leaves that one in the care of a pastor.

The pastor says, "Good. You are on fire. That is awesome. Let us see what we can do with this fire. Let me teach you what to do."

He says things like, "Do you know that you should not be doing this in the world? Do you know that if you want to walk in blessing that you should be applying this to your life?" That is why the pastor needs to be able to teach as well.

He needs to be able to instruct and heal. If you are having problems in your marriage, he will see how you can use the power of God to deal with those problems. Then slowly, they will become mature as an individual in Christ. You can do that.

However, in being able to do that you need to have both pastoral functions. You need firstly to be appointed.

UNDERSTANDING THE POSITION OF OVERSEER

Chapter 02 – Understanding the Position of Overseer

When Moses decided that he would take on the Egyptians before God had appointed him, the Israelites said, "Who do you think you are to come and tell us what to do?"

Yet, when God sent him back with His authority, it was something entirely different. He stood up there with his staff and the elders listened because he had received authority. You are going to learn that authority is delegated downwards, starting from the apostle.

Delegation of Authority

That is why the apostles appointed the elders. The authority is always passed down. Even in the natural we have a need to know where we stand. Somebody can be extremely anointed, but if you do not have a relationship with them in some way, then you are not going to receive that anointing.

You have to come under the authority of that person to receive what they have. In the other hand, before anyone is going to receive from you, you need to stand in authority. You need to stand as an elder, overseer or leader.

If you have been going through leadership training and the Lord has been challenging you on your weaknesses, then it is good, because pastoral training is included with much leadership training as well.

This is because one of the main functions of the pastor is to lead. We know about the pastor's heart. We know about the mending, counseling and typical functions of the pastor, but what about the elder and overseer part? What about the ability to lead God's people?

Anointed to Lead

It takes an anointing, but it also takes a delegation from an authority that is above you. That is why it has to come from the apostle. When we look at that, we can see why there is a huge gap in the church right now.

It is because the church is full of self-appointed elders. Where did they get their authority from? Then, they cannot understand why they get so far and no further. It is because they are limited in the authority that they have.

Moses appointed leaders of fifties, hundreds and thousands. Those that were leaders of thousands had a bit more punch than those that were leaders of fifties. Yet, at the end of the day, where did any of them get their authority from? They got it from Moses.

Where did Moses get his authority from? It was delegated downwards from the Lord. If one of those leaders of fifty judged a case according to the law and it was not obeyed, he referred that person to the leader of a hundred.

Then, if he did not listen to that leader, it would be escalated to the leader of one thousand. After that, if he still did not receive it, then they take it to Moses.

Of course we had someone by the name of Achan that did not even listen to the word Moses gave.

At that time Joshua had taken over the position of Moses. So, Joshua said, "Ok Lord. He is all yours." Rather listen to the leader of fifty. Take my word on this one. Achan came to know that day the price to be paid for not submitting to God's authority! (Joshua 7)

Finding Your Place

I have seen throughout the process of training, that God starts applying pressure to you through the person immediately over you. When that does not work He takes it higher.

Do not find yourself in the hands of God. King David did that and the Lord said to him, "Are you going to run from your enemies for so long or are you going to have me smite the people?" (2 Samuel 24: 13)

David said, "Let me fall upon the hand of God." How many tens of thousands of people died? You do not want to find yourself before the hand God.

You can only have confidence as an elder or a leader when you are in that delegated authority.

The best part about understanding your place in authority is that you have the rest that the position gives. You do not have to fight for your position. When leadership or authority is delegated downwards, you do not have to fight for it because it has been delegated to you.

If you do not like it, we can take it up a level. Would you like to take it up a level and go to the overseer of the church? Do you not want to listen to the overseer of the church? Then, let us take it to the overseer of the region.

Don't want to listen to the overseer of the region? That is fine. Then, we can go straight to headquarters and take it to the apostle. Now, you do not want to listen to the apostle either? Well then, let us take it to God.

As a leader, that brings rest because you know where you belong in the chain of command - you do not have to fight for yourself. That is another major problem in the body of Christ, every overseer or pastor stands alone.

The Failure of Standing in Your Own Authority

Everyone is standing in their own authority, so where does he have to go to when he has problems with his congregation? He has to stand in front of the pulpit saying that they must obey him and do what he says.

When you are in a relationship with other fivefold ministers, you do not have to stand up and say, "Look at me. I look good." No. The pattern, (As we apply it in our ministry), is to stand up and say, "This team member stands in the fullness of their office. Treat them as you would me. I have delegated my authority to them!"

Isn't this what Paul did for both Timothy and Titus? He told the churches, "If anyone asks about Titus – he is my co-worker, so show him love." (2 Cor 8)

He says to the Corinthian Church of Timothy, "He will remind you about my way of doing things… and I am coming there shortly and if you are being arrogant, I will sort you out!" (1 Corinthians 4)

Both Titus and Timothy could step out in the fullest of confidence, knowing that their delegated authority covered them.

The Joys of Delegated Authority

I started out in ministry so young. I preached "Prophetic Child" when I was around twenty-one. Everyone said that I looked like a college kid. (These days, I wish they still would still say that! Reality check though… time has moved on.)

Do you know what the best thing was back then though? As I rose up, my father gave me some of his authority and if I had a problem with anybody, I could say, "Let us take this to a higher authority."

Before I stood up to lead, my father would prepare the way by letting people know that his seal was on me. My authority was delegated.

It was just like David did with Solomon. He got all the leaders together and said, "I want you to take note of my son Solomon. He is young and immature, but I want you to support him.

I am giving him my mantle and scepter and he is going to rule and build the temple." (1 Chronicles 29)

He was even a bit gutsy. He told them to bring him their money so that he could give it to his son and his son can build the temple of God.

He said, "You better submit and obey because I am putting him in charge just as God has told me."

Solomon did not have to stand up as a conquering hero and push his way and neither did Joshua.

Moses presented Joshua to the people. There is a rest in that. When we look at delegated authority and that position of an overseer, you can immediately see where you fit into the pattern.

There comes a rest because you do not have to do it all yourself. Authority is delegated. We look at the story of the centurion who sends his servant to Jesus and he says, "Master, my servant is sick."

The Pharisees were going on about what a good man this was. So Jesus said, "Ok. I will come." On the way, the servant comes to Jesus and says, "Master, I am not worthy to have you in my house. However, I am a man that is under authority and when I say to this man or that man go, they go. (Matt 8:8)

Therefore, I know that when you speak, your servants will go. Jesus said, "Never have I seen a man with such faith in all of Israel." This man knew the power of authority. It is a rest.

The Rest Under Authority

That centurion knew that just as he was in charge over certain men and they would obey him, Jesus was the same way. He had that same authority in the earth. He had authority over sickness, demons, and everything else.

He knew that if Jesus spoke, it would be like him giving a command because of the authority that had been delegated to Him from the Father. It is such a simple, but profound revelation.

When we see that, we see how powerful the pastor can really be. What incredible potential. If we had pastors spending more time on their ministry function because they were already in a rest concerning their leadership function, then we would see magnificent growth in the Church.

Yet, our pastors have to spend so much time trying to prove themselves to people that they do not have time to minister unhindered. It is because they are not under authority.

Fivefold Ministry Overseers

Now you will notice that there were varied levels of overseers in the Scriptures. They may have started out as elders because of their natural maturity and leadership skills, but as time progressed, we see many varied overseers finding their place.

They started out doing the jobs of pastors, and from there, they developed into prophets, teachers, and apostles.

So, let us look at the ministry function now. We have a very clear picture of delegated authority by man and this aspect of pastoral ministry. I just want to mention that this authority will change from ministry to ministry.

Those submitted to Peter followed him exclusively and those submitted to Paul followed them exclusively. Sure, they worked together, but Timothy was directly under Paul's authority.

We know that Titus was directly under Paul's authority too, because Paul said to him, "I am sending you out to go and appoint the elders as I have appointed you." He did not mess with Peter's people and Peter did not mess with Paul's people.

Even though they wrote the same New Testament and did the same work, they had separate mandates. Therefore, they passed down the authority that God had given them as apostles to those under them.

Apostolic Authority Passed Down

Unfortunately, since Peter did not do as much writing as Paul, we see more of what Paul did than Peter. Clearly, Paul had authority because we see over and over how he sent people out.

He sent Silas and Timothy ahead or left them behind to finish up a work. Either that or he told them to come and join him once they were finished with something else. He would even say, "You receive my son who I am sending and you treat him as you would treat me."

He sent him in his authority. I am sure that he received revelation from God as an apostle of who to send and what to do, but the point is that he said to the people, "I am sending you this person and you will listen to him."

That is the picture. That is certainly what we do in our ministry. That gives me the greatest joy as a leader. We can say, "We are sending this person to you and you need to obey and submit as if we were talking, because God has a purpose here. You receive from them."

You do not have to fight for your position. It is given to you on a silver platter.

THE PATTERN FOR THE PASTOR

Chapter 03 – The Pattern for the Pastor

Numbers 11:24 – 25

> *So Moses went out and told the people the words of the Lord, and he gathered the seventy men of the elders of the people and placed them around the tabernacle.*
> *25 Then the Lord came down in the cloud, and spoke to him, and took of the Spirit that was upon him, and placed the same upon the seventy elders; and it happened, when the Spirit rested upon them, that they prophesied, although they never did so again.*

In the previous chapters, we got a good look at our elders as mentioned in this passage. These were the seventy guys that were the top elders. God got them together after Moses picked them out, and although Moses picked them, it was the Lord that put the anointing on them.

Your Position is Determined by Man's Authority

Something important to remember about being an elder is that your position as an elder depends on where your function lies. For example, if you are an elder in our ministry or whatever church you are with, then you have that position of leadership because it is given by man.

However, if you left that organization, you cannot still be an elder in someone else's church.

Now the ministry is something completely different. That goes with you no matter what position you are in.

Your Ministry is Determined by God's Anointing

That is something that God has anointed you with. If you do not feel like leading one day, it does not mean that the anointing has suddenly left. The anointing comes and it remains.

That is the ministry function that God has given the pastor, to lay down the law in the hearts of God's people. That is the day to day stuff. Leading people is not just about being out front. That is only one aspect of the pastoral calling.

When the shepherd stands, the sheep follow behind. Then, he leads them to the pasture and he sits and he lets them eat. There he will tend the lambs and help the sheep give birth.

Being the Shepherd

He will look to make sure that they have water and if they break a leg or hurt something - he is there for them. He protects them from the wolves and takes care of them. However, first he leads them to that place and then he ministers to them.

What a beautiful picture that God has given us of the function of the pastor. It is to feed the sheep and lead them to still waters. It is to go and minister. That is why that pastoral office, (or ministry appointment if you will) can only be given by the Lord.

You can be appointed as an elder, but that does not mean that you have the anointing. That is given by God alone. Put the two together and you will have a pastor.

Appointment + Anointed = Pastor

A pastor is someone who is capable to stand up and be such a strong leader that the sheep will follow. Yet, what happens when they get there? That is what makes or breaks a good shepherd.

It is so easy to stand up and have the sheep follow you when you are taking them to the still waters or to the grassy patch where they can feed. That is not the hard work. The hard work is the stuff they do the rest of the day.

The hard work is that one little prophetic sheep. Those are the ones that run around with their heads in the clouds. All the other sheep are going one way and the prophetic sheep is going somewhere else, and the next thing you know he is falling off a cliff again.

Then, you must go and get the prophetic sheep that has fallen off the ledge again... that is when the real work begins.

Bringing It Together

To stand up and have the sheep follow you to the destination is easy.

To sit down and feed, nurture, take care of the sheep, make sure everything is ok, and find the lost sheep is the hard work. That is the ministry of the pastor.

When you put the two pastoral functions together, I start getting excited at what we are going to see in the body of Christ.

We have some good, strong leaders, but if we add the ministry aspect, then we will have good, strong leaders that will mature the body of Christ.

We have those that are so strong in the Lord and powerful in ministry, but they are lousy leaders who have not been delegated a position. Because of that, no one listens to their message.

They may have a beautiful paradise to show the sheep, but no one wants to follow them there. I am sure that you have felt that way sometimes. You think, "Lord, I have all this truth, teaching, and a heart to reach your people. Why are you not opening the way?"

It is because you have left out an important aspect of pastoral ministry - which is leadership. Where is your authority? Who has it been delegated from? Have you been put in place so that you can pour out that ministry and grow in your ministry?

You Need Sheep to be a Shepherd

You can have all the pasture in the world and even daisies, flowers, lakes and rivers, but if you have no sheep, then it is a waste of time. It is a lonely picnic out there.

Unfortunately, let us be honest, out of all the fivefold ministry, the prophets are the guiltiest of this. They want to go "out there" and have a "dance hallelujah" time in the fields. That is great, but who is following you out there?

You are having a glory-hallelujah with the Lord and then you come down from heaven and find that you are all alone. What happened to the sheep?

Moses took the elders with him half way up the mountain. They could not go with him all the way, but they went up high enough so that they could see and touch the glory of God. Moses could not bring that glory down all by himself. He needed the elders to help distribute some of that glory.

The Pastor in the Local Church

When you look at that, you see the function of the pastor in the local church. The pastor in the local church is found where the people live. It starts with one person.

Remember how I taught you about the local church and how it starts with two cells, then goes to three cells and four cells? That is all you need. The pastor starts right there with someone that has a heart for the Lord and he takes that fire and nurtures it.

He is the one that says, "I understand." He is the one that picks up the phone and says, "I heard that you got into an accident. I heard that something happened." He calls to say, "I miss you."

Spot the Pastor

Look around for people that others follow. You will see that they are the ones that have a heart for God's people. It is those that want to feed, nurture, be there with patience and listen to their long, boring stories for hours at a time. Right there, you have a pastor.

Encourage that person because that is a future leader. That is somebody with the potential to rise up. All they need is some training, hope, and motivation and they can become a leader of fifty, hundreds, or thousands.

They are going to be your elders in the local church. Let us make it really practical.

A Growth Dynamic

Let us say that you have a local church of ten people right now. You have a church in your home and you are doing some bible studies and then there is this one guy that seems to have a heart for the people. As you look closer, you see that everyone looks up to him.

What you have there is an elder. What you need to start doing is pulling this guy aside and train him. You need to encourage the people to look up to him.

You start making this guy look good. You say, "How about you preach this week? I want you to share." Then, you tell people to listen to him and things will happen naturally after that.

Those that are drawn to him are the ones that are supposed to be under his leadership. When it gets too big, then you know it is time to split. You tell him to take the people that are drawn to him and you take the rest.

Perhaps, you have two that rise up and you can split the group each way. Then, what do you do? You have just become a leader of fifty because you have multiplied yourself. Then, you take those two elders that you trained up and be their pastor.

Becoming a Leader of Thousands

They will come to you once a week and say, "Man, I had a really rough week. I have this person that went back to drugs again." Another one will say, "A doctrinal question came up that I did not have the answer for. How do I handle this?"

Then, you come as the elder or leader and say, "Have you tried this? Have you thought about that?" It is so simple.

Perhaps the Lord leads you to attend a seminar and you are all fired up because of the new principles you just learned. What is the first thing that you should do when you get home?

You should get your elders together and say, "Guys, I have something to teach you. I have some apostles' doctrine for you." It said that in the early church they got together and broke bread and received the apostles' doctrine on a daily basis.

Passing on the Apostle's Doctrine

How do you think that the apostles' doctrine got around? It was something that had to be fed again and again, piece by piece. They swapped letters around all over the place. Paul would say, "Make sure this church reads it and that church reads it."

Do you think that every church member got a copy? Certainly not. Not in that age. The elders got it. Then, they passed it down to the people.

So, you receive this great teaching and you get your elders together and you show them the video and you go through it with them and then they will pass it on to the people.

You do not need to have twenty meetings. You just need to have one. Then, those elders' works will start to grow. Their group of six will suddenly become a group of twelve or fifteen. Then, what are you going to tell them?

You are going to say, "Do you remember what I did with you? I want you to look out for the guy that everyone is looking up to. Start pulling him aside and spend some extra time with him."

Start teaching and training him and the next thing you know, that group will be splitting and you will become the leader of one hundred. How else are you going to grow your ministry?

This is the way. You find your elders and let them do the work because it is what burns in them. Then, you continue with those leaders, and as more elders are appointed and they start to grow, you get them together and you impart everything you have.

Delegating Your Authority

It flows from the head down. There is something about having someone that has a vote of confidence in you. You do not want to let them down. I know that everyone, especially if you are a leader in the body of Christ has had a challenge with someone in leadership.

What is the greatest challenge that you had with them? It is that they just did not trust you. Let us be honest. They did not believe in you and that hurt more than anything else.

They did not have a vote of confidence that said, "I trust you so much that I am going to put my sheep in your care and I am going to make sure that they stay in your care because I believe in what God has put in you."

They did not say, "I want you to know that I want you to grow and I want you to come to me and I will continue to impart to you so that you do continue to grow." You will not easily turn your back on such a leader.

Have you asked the Lord why you have seen so many churches face a dramatic split? Harsh words are spoken. One half of the church goes one way and the rest another. You wonder what you did and why it had to happen. The principle that I am sharing with you right here is God's growth dynamic.

It is a law that He set into the Church and either you follow it, or you do not... either way that split is coming! Now you can go through the agonizing experience of having it torn from you, or you can learn to let go and trust God.

You can pre-empt the harsh words and broken hearts by picking out those leaders and giving them a vote of confidence. Now I cannot promise that they will always follow under your care. I cannot promise that they will not eventually go their own way, taking your sheep with them.

However, I can promise you this – it is going to happen either way. So you can participate in this process with joy or you can be crushed when your arm is twisted. The Church has seen enough torn congregations, so instead of it being a travail, why can't it be a celebration of birth?

If you do it right, the elder you raise up will be under your authority and if anything goes wrong in his church, he knows that you have his back. There comes a mutual respect and a relationship of trust, faith, hope, and love. This work will not be based on a pattern or the law, but on the Spirit of Christ.

Trusting the Holy Spirit

The Holy Spirit brings unity to the point where all of us are flowing in the same spirit, having the mind of Christ. The kind of place where He is bringing maturity to every man so that we can be fully equipped to do good works of every kind.

How are we going to reach the body of Christ trying to do it alone? I can take a handful of coals and work that flame. The cool thing about having a handful of coals is that when you have a fire that is going out or needs more life, all you need to do is take a few of those coals and put them in the fire.

Then, you can start bringing it to life again and we can start ministering to the body of Christ and spread this fire out. We can spread the warmth over the whole church. That is the function of the elder in the local church.

The Early Church Pastoral Example

When we look at the early church, we see the pattern so clearly. The apostles did not sit and play church. They went and appointed elders. Then, there were times when you could see that Apostle Paul went and spent time with guys like Priscilla and Aquila and Apollos.

He poured into them and mentored them. He spent time with Silas, Timothy, and Titus. He spent extended time with them and when the time was right, He sent them out.

Then, what did he do? He continued laying down the law. He continued to write doctrine. The enemy thought that he would snatch him up and throw him into prison and stop the work, but guess what? He wrote letters and continued preaching the doctrine.

The Apostle Working With Elders

Then, what happened to that doctrine? It was passed down to the elders, which was passed down to more elders, and then more elders, so that no matter if you were the smallest part of the body of Christ, you got to hear the apostles' doctrine.

He had such a close relationship with each one, that when he was on his way to Rome and he stopped off at one of the beaches there, he got together with all the elders and said, "Guys, I am not going to see you again.

This is it. I am going to strengthen you in the Lord and then it is goodbye."

The Word says that they wept on him because they knew that they would not see his face anymore. They loved Paul. He was their father. That is why he said, "You have many teachers, but not many fathers."

You do not have many parents in Christ that will take the time to invest in you. I am sure that you know what it is like for others not to have a vote of confidence in you. The question is, are you going to make the same mistake or are you going to give others a vote of confidence and say, "You can do it. In fact, I am giving you some of my authority."

Having Courage to Delegate

When you know that you have messed up so badly and your leader still says, "If that is what they said then I back them up one hundred percent, because when they stand up they stand in my authority and whatever they say is what I say." As a leader, that is very humbling.

That is the great thing about having those different levels of authority. As an elder you know that the elder over you will support you, but if those people are out of line we must not forget that there is a rod of correction in the body of Christ as well.

On one hand, I defend each of my team righteously in front of the people, when they mess up. Yet, on the other hand, there are times that I need to go to them and say, "Explain to me why this person is not walking in faith? Explain to me why there is deception in this ministry? Explain to me why this person is completely out of order?"

I need to say, "Why have you not dealt with it?" As a leader, they are responsible for those under them.

Paul said, "I have been hearing that there is one among you that has been living a life of sin. Why has this one not been corrected?" He did not preach to that man, he spoke to the leadership! (1 Cor 5:1)

He said, "Why have you, leaders, not done something about it? What is your problem? This is what you should have done."

He took the leaders to task, not the person. Then, once the man had done what the leaders told him to do, Paul said, "I believe he has repented. Let us bring him back into fellowship."

He held the leaders responsible and in the same way as an overseer, you will be held responsible. You are held responsible before God as overseers of the flock.

James – Our Model of the New Testament Pastor

Jesus released Peter to go and feed the sheep and the next thing you know James is in charge. Where did James come from? You do not even hear about James in Jesus' entire ministry and then all of a sudden he is a big name amongst the Early Church leadership.

Then, you have Barnabas who is the leader at Antioch. Who were they? They were the pastors. They are a picture of what the pastor looks like in the universal church.

When there was a problem about the Gentile Christians being pressured to submit to the Jewish law, guess what they did? They went to headquarters. They went to James. Then, James and the apostles got together and decided what the doctrine or law was going to be and then they filtered it down to the rest of the church.

James worked with the church on a daily basis. He was not out there evangelizing and breaking new ground. He was working with believers who had been saved for years and he said to them you cannot just pray and say, "Be fed."

He was upset that believers were going home hungry after meetings. He told them that they needed to give the people some food and to have acts that proved their faith.

He was the one to deal with all practical church issues. He was speaking to believers who had been saved for some time and he had to bring them to maturity.

He said to the elders, "What is this nonsense? How about you put some works with your faith." They were getting a little holier than thou. They just wanted to pray that God would provide the needs for their brother and have a big glory hallelujah time, while the man went home starving. (James 2)

He said, "Let us see some action. Let us see some works with that faith." That is because he worked with real people and anyone that has worked in a local church knows what I am talking about.

Getting Real

We are all so quick to pray and very slow to put our hands in our pockets. We are so slow to put some action to our prayers. James was dealing with that all the time. It was not that he did not understand or believe in the grace of God, he was just telling the people that they were taking advantage of the grace of God.

He was telling them to include a bit of reality and to bring heaven to earth. That is why he challenged them on the way that they spoke and acted because the world was looking at them. Their tongues were spreading fires and they were not good fires.

He told them to tame their tongue and shut up from time to time. I tell that to the prophets all the time. It is not about learning to speak, but about learning to shut up. James knew that.

When you look at his book from this perspective, it makes so much sense because he was the resident pastor. That is how he fulfilled the function of a pastor-teacher and an overseer.

Together, the elders and the apostles laid down the pattern, the rules and regulations for the church.

Who is Your Pastor?

I want to end this chapter with a question.

Who is your pastor and who are you pastoring?

If you are in ministry, you are a pastor and you are under a pastor. For me, my husband is my pastor. When I have a need, problem or stress, I go to him. He counsels, teaches, and helps me.

Who is your pastor? We get so hung up on discipleship, spiritual parenting, and this and that, and if you are outside of the church you just want to kick out the whole "pastor thing" all together.

So, who is your overseer and who are you overseeing? Where are you in this ladder of command? If you are not in one, then you better find one because it comes down from the apostle and ultimately the Lord Himself.

Do you have the picture in your mind yet? Who is your pastor and who are you pastoring? Find your place.

Open your heart and let the glory flow just as it flowed down from the mountaintop to Joshua to the elders and then to the people. Let the glory begin to flow. You do not need to try to bring the glory or work for the glory.

All you need to do is get in the stream and the glory will come. Why do you think there was such power and unity in the early church? They got in line. Once they got in line, all the Lord had to do was start pouring on the head, and the oil went right down to the feet of Aaron's garment. Not a toe was left untouched.

Do not stop the glory of God because you are stepping out on your own and are trying to get your own glory. Why make it so difficult? Just get where the glory is, and just be who God has called you to be.

IDENTIFYING TODAY'S PASTOR

Chapter 04 – Identifying Today's Pastor

Without the anointing all you have as a pastor, is a leadership position. It takes a lot more than delegated authority to get the job done. It takes an appointment from man and from God. If all you have is the appointment of man, you are not a pastor – you are simply a leader in the Church.

To fulfill the true purpose of a pastor, you will need the gifts of the Spirit and the anointing – just like any other fivefold ministers.

The next couple of chapters focuses entirely on the ministry function of the pastor and the place you need to fulfill to mature the Church!

There is an essential need in every single one of us to feel like we belong. I do not think I fully understood this until I went into ministry and God started bringing us spiritual children.

I was pretty blessed. I already had spiritual parents and I grew up in an environment where I had a place where I belonged. I knew that I had a calling and although I had my rebellious years, I was pretty blessed by the fact that I knew that there was light at the end of the tunnel.

Now, I did not always like that light, or want that light, but I knew that it was there when I was ready for it. I knew that there was a track for me to run on. No matter how far I ran from God, I knew that somewhere along the line, I would find my way.

That is because I always had a place to belong. I had parents that taught me that I belonged. However, I came to realize as God raised Craig and I up that there are so many in the church that struggle with so many things.

I see those that have been abused, I see some that have a fire for ministry and do not know where to express it, and I see those with problems and struggles in their marriage and other parts of their lives.

Then, you get into ministry thinking that you can meet all those needs in others. You can cast out all the demons, deal with the addictions, and bring victory, but at the core of every problem and every person that we came across, we saw this one thing – a need to belong.

When we met that one simple need, all the other problems took a back seat and seemed to solve themselves overnight.

A lot of the struggle that we have is not in lacking the boldness to do what we need to do. We have the fire and we know that we need to step out and speak. However, we need someone to be on our side of the court saying, "You are completely normal."

A Place to Belong

When you have that, you have the courage to face your sin and any storm that comes your way. In fact, we came to experience that just giving people a place to belong and meeting that simple need, brought about more deliverance than you can imagine.

And so, God started bringing us people from all over. You can see our team now, but you do not know what they looked like when they first arrived to us. You know what I am talking about if the Lord has sent you spiritual children.

I said, "Lord, do you have the right address? Are you kidding me? I cannot minister to these people. I do not have the first clue. I feel like I had a bit of a sheltered upbringing to be honest. How do I minister?"

The Lord said to me, "Give them a place to belong. Just love them."

It was miraculous. From that, everything else in our ministry was born. From that single principle, deliverance and healing (physical, emotional, or spiritual) was born. Imparting the gifts of the Spirit was so easy from there and impartation of the anointing was instantaneous.

So often, we try to add the gifts of the Spirit and the ministries, but they do not stick. It is like trying to put a sticky note on the fridge, but the stickiness is gone and it keeps falling off.

Nothing works because of this essential need - the need to belong. They need to have a place of peace and rest, and have the ability to just be who they are.

I bet that if I had to ask you to tell me the last time that you were able to just be who you are, there are not many times that you are going to be able to think of - married or not.

Where can you just be, and not perform, be something, do something, be somewhere, or prove yourself? Where can you not have to get people to listen to you or agree with you, but you can just be who you are with all of your junk?

If we could find this place, this person... everything else would come together. Once we fill that essential need in our hearts, the gifts, the ministries, our calling, the boldness and courage that we need, will all no longer be a problem.

You see, I can have the courage to stand up and do all the things that I do, because I know that I have a place where I belong. When all is said and done and all the lights are off and I am not in my high heels anymore, I can just be who I really am.

Since, I can be who I really am in my secret place, I can be who I really am when I stand up front as well. Who I am is acceptable in my secret place, and it is also acceptable in public. So, I can be real with everyone when I stand up in public.

Making the Church a Place to Belong

It is the pastor who brings this place to the church, at least it should be. That is the essence of what a pastor is called to do and be. The pastor is meant to give the church a place to belong so that we might flourish.

Then, we might have the courage to evangelize and get the healing that we need in our marriages. We will also have the boldness to go out and do what God has called us to do, and mend relationships with our children and families.

We will then be a city on a hill, flowing in all the gifts of the spirit and not bogged down with all of our preconceived ideas of sin, shame, and guilt. All of these things are like walls around the anointing that God is trying to flow through us as a Church.

I am not even talking about leaders here - I am talking about believers as a whole. The anointing is within them, but they cannot flow out because they have so many hurts and struggles.

Then, amongst all that, they are trying to perform and prove to everyone so that they can get that deep need met. Unfortunately, what has happened is, instead of coming to the church and the pastor, they are going to pornography sites and gambling to get those needs met.

Let's be clear - I am not talking about unbelievers here, let's not be naïve. That craving that you feel inside leads you to places that you should not go to, and that craving is a need to belong, to be accepted as you are.

God, in these end-times, is raising up true pastors who are creating such an environment in the Church. When the Church realizes that it belongs, has a purpose, and has a place for healing, then there will be no stopping the fire that will come out from the Church.

You may just have a small flame, a tiny candle, but if we can get that one flame to burn in each and every one of us, and we put our lights together and put them on top of that hill, we are going to have an inferno.

However, the only time that candle is going to burn in our hearts, is when we are comfortable enough to let it burn. We all have the desires and passions that excite us, that we have never told other people about.

These are exciting things that light a fire in you, but you are too ashamed to talk about them. You think, "I cannot do that. I am not capable."

However, what if we found you a place where you were ok with letting go of all of your excuses, letting go of all your hurts and pains from the past? I would not need to tell that fire to come out because it would come out naturally.

I see this in homes. When parents give their children a place to belong and they accept them as who they are, you do not need to tell the children to be confident.

You do not have to tell those children to be passionate about life. They just are, because they belong. When that need is met in them, all the passion, desire and vision come out naturally.

It is about time that we start seeing that in the church. God has put something special in each and every believer, and it is indeed the role of the pastor to nurture, pull out, and blow on the flame when it starts to go down.

It is the pastor's role to say, "I know that you are a lousy, big mouth, and you mess things up. You prophetic types go and say things that you should not. Let's calm you down and give you some healing to those hurts of the past and then let's work with that fire.

Let's get to the place where just the fire comes out and not all the rest with it."

It takes a pastor, a very special ministry, to do this. I am not talking about someone who is just good with people. It does not mean that because you are good with people that you are going to be a pastor.

I guarantee that God is going to call you to be a pastor if you are not good with people. God said to me, "Colette, I have called you to love my people and to be a spiritual mother."

I said, "Lord, do you not need somebody nice for that? You should ask Craig. He is so nice."

When we would go out, people always said, "Your husband is so friendly. He is such a nice guy." They never said that about me.

Just because you are nice, that does not mean that you are a pastor. We make the mistake of thinking that because you are a big mouth and you talk a lot that you naturally are a prophet, or if you are nice, quiet, and nurturing, then you are a pastor.

No, this is not a natural gift. It is an anointing. It is going to take a lot more than being nice to create an environment where people feel like they belong. It is going to mean becoming a spiritual parent.

You are going to need a pattern, plan and a calling. That is the calling of the pastor.

The Pastoral Calling

Now, when I say this word, all the prophets start triggering and I see manifestations, roots of bitterness, and judgments coming out. If I ever want to insult a prophet and give them a back hand to their mouth, I just say, "God has called you to be a pastor."

It is because of what they have experienced. However, I am trying to separate what you see as the position of pastor, and what is indeed the ministry of a pastor. It takes a lot more than a position to be a pastor.

It takes a calling and an anointing to be a pastor. I shared in Today's Evangelist how he is who he is because of the anointing. It is the same for the pastor. Yes, much like the evangelist, the word "pastor" has been used very loosely used in the Church.

Tradition dictates that if you have a church, you are a pastor. This is not necessarily true. I have seen a lot of evangelists that have home church meetings and even prophets starting churches. However, this position is what the world recognizes as a reverend, a leader, or a shepherd.

Now, in many ways, they are still pastors because the pastor has a two-fold function. One is positional and one is ministerial. Right now, I want to look specifically at the ministerial function of the pastor.

I want to share about the role that he plays to minister and the anointing that he flows in. You prophets are about to get a little bit surprised.

Pastoral Prophets?!

Could it be that God has been trying to raise you up as a pastor before you move into your prophetic ministry? There is a whole big chunk that you are missing. I was a prophet of prophets. I would stand up and give it to people.

Go watch my early prophetic videos. You will see that I hardly sit still. There was spitting and spewing and "Die Already" and a whole lot going on there. I was pumped and ready to train the prophets.

When we started our first prophetic school in 1999, I was the first principal and ready to jump into the training aspect when God said, "I need you to pastor my prophets."

I said, "Can I just tell them to die already? I really want to tell them to die already, Jesus."

He started to help me to understand a few things. He said,

"My prophets need a place to belong. Do you not understand that? Since this is a misunderstood call, they have not found a place where they feel accepted and they can let down the guard enough for you to deal with the junk.

If you go in with guns blazing, you are just going to get the same wall that they give to every other pastor and leader out there. They are going to see you coming from a mile away and they are going to feel threatened. They need to feel comfortable and Colette, they need to like you. You need to be nice."

You think you had it tough. I had to be nice to a bunch of prophets that acted just like me! I did not want to be nice. I wanted to kill their flesh and put them on the cross.

However, the crazy thing was that when I could let my need to be heard and need to get my point across go and just love and accept them, and nurture the fire that they had, they ended up beating me to the cross.

I did not need to say, "Die already." They knew what they needed to do already. In fact, I found that the nurturing was a greater incentive to let go of the flesh.

This is the mistake a lot of leaders make when a prophet comes to their door with all of their baggage. They are trying to so hard to prove their call. They put on a double portion of arrogance to try to get their message out and get people to hear them.

Then, they cannot understand why they get knocked down. It takes a pastor to see somebody like that, an evangelist like that, a prophet like that, or anyone like that, and to see through those masks that they have, give them a place to belong and create such a comfortable environment that they let that guard down naturally.

When you find a place where you are loved and where you belong, it is easy to let go of your baggage. You feel secure and you do not think that this certain person is going to take advantage of you.

Where it all began

God is raising up true pastors in this day and age. I came to the Lord and said, "Where did it begin?" I know that we are looking at *Today's Pastor*, so I wanted to know where "yesterday's pastor" is mentioned in the Word.

As a teacher, I want to know the "why" and "how long?" The main point that I wanted to know was where did the pastoral ministry come from?

Ephesians 4 and 1 Corinthians 12 lays it all out, but that was not good enough for me. I wanted to know where it started. The Lord pointed me to a very interesting scripture that ties in so beautifully.

The Old Testament Pastor

It started in Exodus 19 where the Lord birthed a nation.

> *Exodus 19:4 You have seen what I did to the Egyptians, and how I bore you on eagles' wings and brought you to Myself.*
> *5 Now therefore, if you will indeed obey My voice and keep My covenant, then you shall be a special treasure to Me above all people; for all the earth is Mine.*
> *6 And you shall be to Me a kingdom of priests and a holy nation.' These are the words which you shall speak to the children of Israel.*

The Lord gave them a place to belong. He birthed a nation and drew them to Mount Sinai and it was here that Israel was truly born. Yes, the Lord had the covenant with Abraham, Isaac, and Jacob, but they were not really considered a proper nation, until the encounter where Moses went up the mountain and got the book of the Law.

The Birth of a Nation

The Lord then started structuring things. You can study this in any nation. I am busy taking my son through American history and how all the colonies came into being. Who knew there was so much to learn about America?

When did America really become a nation? Was it when people first landed here?

There were groups of people all over the place. America only became a nation when they got together, put the law in place, and signed the Constitution.

Once that was done, America considered themselves a nation. That is what God did for the children of Israel. He brought them to Mount Sinai. Up until then, there were twelve tribes.

There was a little bit over here and little bit over there, a colony here and a colony there, and everyone had their own banners. There was not even any real structure. Everything was recorded mostly by bloodline.

They were the twelve sons of Jacob. That is how it was. Then God said, "Come to the mountain. I will make you a treasure to me."

Is that not a beautiful picture of the pastor? Moses created an environment for them that brought them together and gave them a purpose for the future. "This is why you are here, this is where you are going, and this is how I am going to lead you."

The Israelites were given a beautiful pattern. Moses could not have laid it out any clearer for them. If you have ever gone through the first five books of the Bible, then you have seen everything from how they should dress, how often they should wash, where they should sacrifice and even how marriages should be confirmed.

He laid down the law to the letter. It was a beautiful pattern. Moses got the pattern for the tabernacle and he did not leave a ring on the curtain undone. It was perfect, to the "T."

However, a pattern was not enough. You see, us humans like to stray. We have three little boys at our ministry center and we say to them, "You need to be good. You know the rules of the house. You know that you are not allowed to run up and down the hallway, so that when mommy is preaching it does not sound like thundering elephants upstairs, right?"

"Uh huh."

"You know that you are not going to eat all the candy in the room so that you have a sugar buzz and run in circles, right?"

"Uh huh."

They know the law. They may only be three and five years old, but they know the law. Now while Mom and Dad are there, they obey that law. However, just leave those little guys alone for five minutes and see if they keep that law.

They think, "I know where Mom keeps that chocolate stash. I know that it is against the law, but…"

That is the nature of us humans. They may be really young, but we are no different and neither were the children of Israel. They had the pattern. They knew what they needed to do, but they needed some policemen.

Leadership Set in Place

They needed someone to help maintain that law.

> *Exodus 30:30 And you shall anoint Aaron and his sons, and consecrate them, that they may minister to Me as priests.*

After all was said and done, God set the law and gave the Ten Commandments. He gave the "thou shalts" and "thou shalt nots" and then He said, "Ok, now I need some policemen to police that law and make sure that the law is maintained from generation to generation."

The First Pastors Are Born

So, He called the Levites aside. He said that the Levites would be His inheritance and they would not have land amongst the other Israelites. He made them priests. Ladies and gentlemen, this is where we see the birth of the pastoral ministry.

Right here, you have the priests that maintained the law. If you look at the functions of the priests and what they did in the Old Testament, you begin to get a picture of what God is doing in today's Church.

God's people needed to be reminded. There were a lot of laws going on in the Old Testament. When you had a baby, you had to go out of camp. When you had sex, you had to wash. (I do not want to know what priest maintained that in Israel. That does not sound like a fun job.)

There were cleanliness rites, incense that needed to be burned, and sacrifices that needed to be made. There was a letter and a law that had to be kept up with.

The Conduct of the Priests

You must keep in mind that there was no indwelling of the Holy Spirit. So, they could not "go with the flow" and say, "What do I sense in my spirit today? Let's go and check on those washings and make sure that everyone is keeping nice and pure."

They did not sense what was in the spirit or what to do next. They simply went by the letter of the law. I imagine how that must have been for the priests of the Old Testament.

Have you ever imagined how that must have been for them? Here we are in ministry and we get that unction of the Holy Spirit to preach this, to go here, or to do something, but they did not have that.

Unless the Holy Spirit came upon them from without, causing them to experience something, they really just had to go by the letter of the law. They followed the rules and made sure that everyone else followed the rules too.

Responsibilities of the Priests

The priests had two main purposes. They were to serve God and to serve Israel. They had very specific responsibilities that I am going to quickly share with you.

Took Offerings on Behalf of Others

Firstly, they took offerings on behalf of God's people. That is kind of strange, if you think about it. Imagine if you want to pray and ask the Lord for forgiveness of your sin.

For us, it takes five minutes. We say, "I really should not have said that thing to that driver (that I am still really mad with). Forgive me, Lord. I should not have said or done that."

It is so quick and easy for us. However, in that day and age it was not so quick and easy. If you sinned, you had to go and bring an offering, and the worst part, is that you could not even offer it yourself.

The priests had to be purified and then they would take your offering and present it to the Lord for you. So, you did not even have a relationship with God as an Israelite. You had to rely on the priest to take the offering for you to the altar.

People would come with their sin offerings and when I considered that, I thought, "That is pretty personal."

How many times have you done something that you did not want anyone else to know about, something really personal? You go to the Lord, find a quiet spot, and say, "Lord, I really messed up. Please help me and forgive me."

You know those prayers that I am talking about. Well, these people did not have that option. If they committed adultery or any crime and they wanted forgiveness for that sin, then they had to go to the priest with their sin offering.

They had to say, "Please sacrifice this dove because I slept with my neighbor's wife."

Took Care of the Temple

So, the priests were involved a lot more in people's lives than we realize. They ministered to the Lord, put out the incense, made the daily sacrifices, and very importantly, they tended to the temple.

They were the ones that made sure that it was clean and repaired. When King Jehoash (2 Kings 12:6) came and said, "What is wrong with the temple?" It was the priests that he complained to.

He said, "I have given you the money. Why is it not repaired?"

It was the priest's responsibility to make sure that the house of God was taken care of. Are you starting to see some of the New Testament pastor yet? Are you starting to get this picture?

It is not me that is giving you this picture, but the Holy Spirit that is giving you this picture. As I am sharing, I want you to take more than I am saying. I want you to pick the spirit up and get your own revelation. I want God to put the pieces into your spirit for you.

Taught the Law

Most importantly, they taught the law. Not only did they maintain the law, but they taught it to the people, one by one.

When Ezra and Nehemiah came after rebuilding the temple and the walls of Jerusalem, it says that they stood up front and the priests and the scribes went in amongst the people and retaught the law. (Nehemiah 8)

The people had been away and had just come back to Jerusalem. So, they needed to be retaught the law.

Guess whose job that was? Guess who teaches people the law? The priest or the pastor.

Are you starting to see the function a bit?

Anointed Others to Office

They also anointed others to office. When there was someone that needed to be anointed as high priest or another priest needed to take over, they are the ones that would anoint them and be involved in that process.

It is very interesting that when Solomon was anointed to be king, it was not the prophet alone that anointed him. The priest was there too. Yes prophets... you have to work with a pastor.

They worked together to make the appointment. They did not work solo. The prophet would come in and say, "Solomon is called to be king" or, "David is called to be king."

However, the priests were also very much involved in the coronation ceremony. King Joash was brought to the priests and they appointed him as king and took him through the coronation ceremony. (2 Kings 11)

The priests played a very important role with all the kings that were appointed. Now, there is a little change that starts to happen when you start going through the books written by the prophets. A change we will tackle in the next chapter.

THE TRANSITION TO SHEPHERD

Chapter 05 – The Transition to Shepherd

Up until the book of Jeremiah, it was all about the priests. However, a shift started to take place.

> **Jeremiah 23:4** *I will set up shepherds over them who will feed them; and they shall fear no more, nor be dismayed, nor shall they be lacking,"* *says the Lord.*

Suddenly, out of nowhere, this word "shepherd" came in. It had not been mentioned before. Again, just like I shared on the evangelist, we started seeing a bit of a transition. It was not just about the priests performing service anymore.

From Priests, to Shepherds

What happened at this time was that the priests were really involved in everyone's daily lives and they were the ones responsible to teach the law, so they naturally became leaders.

That is what we see in the time of Jesus as well. They considered the chief priests, chief rulers - as leaders in the community. They started becoming shepherds.

It is obvious that if you are coming to someone with your personal sin and you are looking up to them, you are going to start looking up to them as a leader. Considering that they had to live holier lives and consecrate themselves to the Lord, people would naturally look up to such a person as a model and example.

Is that not why the Lord took Eli to task - because of his sons? They were being a bad example.

So, we see this example and I love the Lord and His Word because we see how He put this nation together. He put all the leadership in place and then as the years developed, we see a maturity taking place within that structure.

We start seeing a progression in those that started out as Levites. Aaron, one of the sons of Levi, became a high priest. Then, later we see those priests rising up in stature within that community and nation, to the point where they were not just servants, but shepherds to the flock.

This word "shepherd" was then carried on through the prophets and they started challenging the priests, not because of their service, but because of their being bad shepherds.

They did not tell the priests that they were doing the sacrifices wrong. They told them that they were being bad shepherds - bad examples. They were being bad models to the children of Israel. That is what God had raised them up to become, just like in today's Church.

This was the start of something new. The Lord was preparing us for the New Testament pastor. The priest of the Old Testament is a type and a shadow. It is not the full picture.

The New Testament

> **Hebrews 8:8, 10** *Because finding fault with them, He says: "Behold, the days are coming, says the Lord, when I will make a new covenant with the house of Israel and with the house of Judah*
>
> *10 For this is the covenant that I will make with the house of Israel after those days, says the Lord: I will put My laws in their mind and write them on their hearts; and I will be their God, and they shall be My people.*

Here is our transition right here. I love this particular chapter in Hebrews because it is all about the high priest of our faith. He speaks about how we needed someone to go and present the sacrifice, but with the coming of Christ, how that changed things up.

We do not just have anyone bringing our sins to the Father anymore. Jesus Himself who was pure in every way, is the one that brings our sins to the Father. We do not have to go to the priests. We can go to Christ.

The New Testament Difference

I love this scripture because it brings the allegory of the pastor to life so much. In the Old Testament, they had to do everything by the book. It was all about the rules. However, now that we have the Holy Spirit, things are not the same. After the day of Pentecost, something changed and they started doing things by the Spirit.

The law was not written on a tablet of stone anymore. The law was not hidden in a book in the Ark of the Covenant anymore. From the day of Pentecost, the Holy Spirit came and He put that law in our minds and hearts.

We received the indwelling of the Holy Spirit and that law is now in us. Was the law abolished? No, the law was implanted. That is what Jesus came to do.

Hebrews 8:13

> *In that He says, "A new covenant," He has made the first obsolete. Now what is becoming obsolete and growing old is ready to vanish away.*

The New Covenant displaced the Old Covenant. I am not saying that it did away with it, but more that it progressed and naturally displaced it. It took the elements, the structure that God had set since the beginning of time, and He added to it His anointing and the indwelling of the Holy Spirit.

Moses had to go up the mountain at least seven times to get the law. He went up and down. He must of have been a pretty fit old man. He had to go high enough that he went into a cloud. That must have been quite the hike.

He did it a number of times. I wonder if they made him a lift eventually!? I am thinking, "Lord, I love you, but really? I need to climb the mountain again?"

Moses would have loved the day of Pentecost. The fire came and there was the law. It is so much easier. It is on our minds and hearts, and it makes everyone's job so much easier.

Position vs. Ministry

What was a ministry of works, is now a ministry of the Spirit. A transition took place when the New Covenant came. Now, position and ministry are two very different things.

In the O. T. priests were appointed by blood and by position. There were some strict laws. You were not allowed to be lame and you had to be perfect in body and mind. There were certain things to abide by, but for the most part, you were appointed just because you were in the right family.

You were given the position because you were born and bred for that position. You did not need any ministry call and what did they need the anointing for? They were just policemen who went by the letter of the law.

They just had to go by the letter of the law and make sure that it was enforced. However, things changed in the New Testament, the law was put on our hearts and now we needed more than just policemen.

We needed someone who could flow by the spirit and let us know which law to use when. We needed someone who could flow with God that we could identify with, that could lead us the way that we needed to go.

We went from getting natural elders (elders meaning those who were mature or away in years), to now being spiritual pastors.

New Testament Comparison

In the Old Testament, if anyone was sick, they went and showed themselves to the priest. If you were afraid that you had leprosy or you had some disease or cough or something you were not sure about, you did not go to the doctor, you went to the priest.

> *James 5:14 Is anyone among you sick? Let him call for the elders of the church, and let them pray over him, anointing him with oil in the name of the Lord*

Before, they went to the priests for this. However, now James is telling them that the dynamics have changed. As Israelites, James and any other Hebrew would have gone to the priests for any sickness.

Yet, James said, "Do not go to the priests. Go to the elders or the pastors. Those are the new priests."

These were not just any old priests. These people were spirit-filled and would be led by the spirit.

They were not people that were obeying the letter of the law, but people that were obeying the spirit of the law.

They were the ones that were going to continue taking this new nation and new covenant that has been birthed and help the people to keep that law.

The Birth of Another Nation

You see, on the day of Pentecost, another nation was born, a peculiar people, a kingdom under God - you and me. He may have established the first nation at Mount Sinai, but on the day of Pentecost He established another nation - a much bigger nation.

This nation was the nation that the Lord was trying to tell them about through all the prophets. He said, "By the way, I am going to have all the Gentiles come to me. By the way, you may be a chosen people right now, but there is a time that is coming when I am going to be available for everyone."

Then, a new nation was born, called the Christian church, on the day of Pentecost and that law was put on our hearts and in our minds and we were filled with the Holy Spirit and with fire.

However, we are still like kids with a candy bar. We know in our spirit that we should not eat the candy bar first thing in the morning because we will get sick, but we really want it anyway.

We need those priests of our faith to say, "You know what your spirit is telling you. You and I both know what God is telling you. Leave that candy bar alone. Get back into church."

We hate that message, but we need those that can maintain the law that God has set and to give us a place to belong.

The Temple – a Place to Belong

You know what I love about the temple? No matter what anyone was going through, there was always a place to belong. Whether you were a beggar on the street or a king in the palace, there was always a place to belong.

That is why the temple was such a big deal, especially in the days of Solomon. It was a gathering place. It was one place where no matter what you did or who you were, if you were an Israelite, you could go there.

There was something about calling yourself an Israelite. There was something about a sense of belonging and being this peculiar people. That is why they were drawn to the temple.

Even when all the apostles started their ministry, what is the first thing that they did? They went to the temple. Why did they do that? It is because that is where everybody was.

It was a hub, signifying the place where they belonged - it connected people.

In this New Testament nation, God has brought us the church and it connects us. It is for the pastors to create this environment, this temple, for us to feel safe and belong to a hub.

This should be a hub where believers can come from all walks of life. You know churches like this. I have seen them. It is a hub where it does not matter if you came from a king's palace or if you are a beggar on the street.

When you come into this place of worship and gather together, this is the place where you belong. It takes a pastor to create such an environment. Can you see why an evangelist would make such a lousy pastor?

What is the first thing that an evangelist is going to do? He is going to preach about sin, your problems, and he is going to bring the fire. That is what the evangelist should be doing. However, if someone is in my face about my innermost sins and secrets, I am not going to let my walls down so easily.

I am not going to open my heart and be vulnerable about how I really feel. I am not letting that hurt out in case he says or sees something that I do not want everyone else to know about.

That is why an evangelist is a great ground breaker, but a lousy pastor. That is why God separated them so clearly for us in the New Testament. Each one has a purpose. Stop jumping all over the place.

Find your purpose and fulfill it. Pastors are so needed in the church today.

In the Old Testament, if you wanted forgiveness of sin, you had to go with your dove, lamb, or whatever you could afford and offer that. I can only imagine how long it must have taken to get forgiveness of sins.

You had to schlep all the way to the temple. You could not even do it in your backyard. You could have had a full schedule for the day, but then you have to go all the way to the temple to make a sacrifice.

Yet, in the New Testament, this is all done through faith. Our forgiveness is now through Christ. What a complete change. With this change, there is a new dynamic and so there was a need for new leaders.

The Lord needed to set some new fivefold ministers in place to be able to take this new nation that He had birthed and give it a structure, a purpose, and a future. That way, we may continue to build, develop, and progress, just like the children of Israel progressed as a nation.

We also need to progress as a nation and not regress. We need to go to higher ground and it is going to take the pastor to do that. If I look in the New Testament, I love the example of James.

James the New Testament Pastor

When you think of James, especially when you read the book of James, you are not seeing the word pastor written all over it. However, if you really are a pastor and you have worked with people the way James worked with people, you will understand him.

You will get him and you feel his heart. Remember how I shared with you that the pastor is not just a "nice" guy. He is not just a nice preacher that is non-confrontational. He is not at all like that.

The pastor will do more confronting than a prophet because he is in people's lives. People let him confront because he loves them enough to get involved in their lives. This is what I see in James.

Martin Luther called this book an epistle of straw. He said, "Where does this book come from with all this emphasis on works?" It came from a pastor that worked with people every day!

He saw their flesh and their sin and he saw how they treated one another and he said,

"We cannot have any more of this. We need unity in the church. We need a place to belong. If we want a place to belong, then you have to treat your brother right.

"For goodness sakes, if the man is starving, do not just say, 'Be fed' and leave him starving. Give him some food. Give him a place to belong. Let him feel accepted. Also, watch what you are saying with your tongue.

"Do you not know that your tongue is a fire, a world of iniquity? You are tearing your brother down. Look what you are doing to each other. Here we are trying to fellowship in the Lord and you guys are destroying one another with your words.

"Let's put that down and embrace one another in love. If you do not love your brother, do not tell me that you love God."

That is the book of James. I love it. I can go on and on about James for hours, but I will spare you.

James taught on day to day matters. He taught on heart matters. He got real deep. He talked about how they ate their food, what they were saying to each other, and how they loved or did not love each other.

He took all these doctrines of Paul, Peter, and whoever else, and he broke it down and made it practical. James did not preach principles, did you notice that? It is real life stuff.

He said, "Don't talk trash. You are full of it and you are striving in your members because you do not have what you want. You do not have what you want because you are asking God for the wrong thing. So, let's just deal with that." (James 4)

It is really in your face and it cuts to your heart. This is real life every day stuff. It is practical. Yes, as a teacher, I love the principles. However, until the principles are lived and applied to the hearts of God's people, all they are... are principles.

The pastor actually goes into the heart and takes the law that has been put there and makes it real. He makes the people live it, and makes it applicable to their life today. James was without a doubt a leader among the elders.

Yes, he was also an apostle, but I want to look specifically at his function as a pastor because I just love that model that he was. He was so strong and confident and he did not mince his words, but still you cannot help but to feel his love for God's people.

So, let's go through this time line and look at the priests who served and the shepherds who led. Let's look at the functions of the priests because when we do that, suddenly, today's pastor will make sense.

Of course, when you add the anointing and the indwelling of the Spirit to that, you will have a whole new picture that starts to come to life. What was law, the Scriptures say, is now a life-giving Spirit.

The law was not dead words anymore. It was not just something written on a scroll anymore. It is something that is alive and real to us.

SIGNS OF TODAY'S PASTOR

Chapter 06 – Signs of Today's Pastor

As with each of the fivefold, the pastoral call comes with signs of its own. You see, the Lord starts to call us not when we feel like it or when we get that anointing one day. Actually, your calling starts way before that.

Your calling started when your mom fell pregnant. In fact, He orchestrated the night of conception they had, so that you can be born.

From that moment, He said, "I am calling this one to be a pastor. I am calling this one to serve in my church. This one is going to be an apostle."

Jesus is the one that calls.

From the time that the sperm met the egg, change started to take place. Everything that happened in your life started to gear you towards where you are today.

God put you where you needed to be to become who you are today. Sure, the devil had a hand in there too. When he sees somebody that is called of God, you can be sure that he is going to get in there.

He is in there saying, "Let me see how I can mess up God's plans." However, God has put the desire in your heart to be who you are today, and then He anoints us when we are ready.

The signs that I am going to share with you are geared specifically for a pastor in office. Just like the prophet and the evangelist have to go through training, so does the pastor. This is something that a lot of people do not realize.

Anointing vs. Position

Many think that the anointing just comes because of the position. This is not the case. Sometimes, the position comes before the anointing comes and sometimes the anointing comes before the position comes.

However, a pastor in office is one that has both. I am zeroing in more on the spiritual side of the pastoral ministry because that is the part that nobody really takes notice of. They just see the position.

They just see the elder, the bishop, the ruler of tens, hundreds, and thousands, but they do not realize that it takes more to be a pastor than just being a strong leader. It takes someone with a pastor's heart and with an anointing.

1. Feels Called to a Community (Stays at Home)

The first sign of a pastor is that he feels called to a community. Throughout all of Israel, the Levites were scattered. If you go and read the Old Testament, you will read how each one of them were sent to different places.

There was a community of priests in each one. They had a portion of land in amongst all the Israelites. They had a community that they worked with. They had a certain group that they worked with.

It is the same with today's pastor. Have you wondered about people that have a heart for a certain place? Often people think that they must be an evangelist, but this is not the case because the evangelist goes out.

However, the pastor is the one that stays at home. He does not have a desire to go out. Do you see what I am saying about the pastor vs. evangelist conflict? The evangelist says, "Let's go out." The pastor says, "Let's stay at home."

If you put these two in the same room, they are going to fight. One of them is going to want to go out while the other wants to stay at home. If you put an evangelist as a pastor of a church, he is never going to be there.

Why Pastors and Evangelists Fight

He is going to be out traveling to all the other churches. What is the point of being a pastor, if you are out traveling? A true pastor is one that stays at home and he is content to set up house.

I know that many people do not like that about the pastor, but has it ever occurred to you that it is what he is meant to be? Give the guy a break. God put that in him since the day that he was born. He cannot shake it.

He feels called to a community. He feels called to a certain kind of people, just like James. James was stuck in Jerusalem and that is where his call was. He ministered to the Jews there.

That is where his heart was and that is why sometimes he was so misunderstood. He also misunderstood Paul. He did not get why Paul was going off to all the Gentiles. Paul was not acting like a good Jew anymore.

James

James must have thought, "What is wrong with you, Paul?" That is because James was zealous for the place that God had put him. That was his church. That was his people and his heart.

Do not expect the pastor to go out. Stop putting pressure on him to go out. He is not meant to go out.

I am a mother. If I left my children all the time to go everywhere, not taking care of my home, and not doing the laundry - what kind of mother would that make me? Not a very good one because it takes a mom to make a home.

It takes a pastor to create an environment where people belong. You cannot create an environment while you are traveling everywhere. That is why it burns in him to stay home and set up house.

He does not like the "scattering thing." He likes the "gathering thing." That is his part to play. Let him play his part and you play yours.

2. Likes Practical Teaching (Breaks Down Doctrine into Practical Teaching)

He likes practical teaching. He breaks down doctrine into steps 1, 2, 3. He explains why you need to know this particular principle. He shows you how it applies to your marriage. He points out how it applies to you as a father or a mother, and how it applies to your workplace.

He is going to talk to you about things that relate to you now and here - today. He wants everyone to understand the major doctrines, but in a way that they can live it right now. A pastor is not someone that is overly impressed with fancy language, and great, big principles.

A real pastor wants you to get the principle. He will break it down as many times as he needs to, until you get it because he wants to see victory in your life. He does not just want you to understand it, but he wants you to know it in your heart and in your mind.

3. Your "Go-To" Person (Gets Involved in Daily Life)

Who is your "go-to" person? I am talking about the person that you go to when you and your spouse get into a fight. Perhaps, you are feeling down and discouraged? There is a person that you go to.

That person is the one who usually understands you and makes you feel comfortable. So then, who is your "go-to" person? If that person is a leader and one that the Lord is raising up, that is likely a pastor that you are looking at.

Since the pastor has this nature to gather and to make people feel at home and comfortable, he is your "go-to" person. He is non-threatening, but he also has the potential to give you a pretty tough word.

He is not going to sugarcoat things for you, but even though he is like that, he is still going to accept you the way that you are.

Sometimes, you maybe deserved a harder word, but He is still the one that you can go to and who gets involved in your daily life.

That is your pastor. I love that sign of the pastoral ministry. So, who is your "go-to" person? Are you the "go-to" person? Does everyone always just tell you their stories?

The Pastoral Anointing Defined

They start saying, "There is this thing that I did and I have never told anyone else about it, but I just feel like I can open up to you."

You think, "Do we know each other? Do I know you? What are you telling me this stuff for?"

I shared in the previous book in this series, Today's Evangelist, that they just stand in the evangelistic anointing and people get saved without them having to say a lot.

Pastoral ministry requires an anointing as well and this is what it looks like. When you get around someone that has this anointing, you just feel a sense of belonging and peace around them.

You do not know what it is about them, but you just feel that you can tell them things that you would not ordinarily tell other people. You do not feel threatened. It is an anointing.

If you are a pastor, people come to you and tell you things that you really rather would not have known about them. I wonder how many of the priests of the Old Testament thought, "I wish you could have sacrificed your own dove today. I have heard it all."

I think that is how the pastor feels sometimes!

4. Gets Personal (Corrects and Encourages)

A pastor gets personal. He corrects and encourages. A pastor gets into your personal space. This is where you become responsible. If you are going to go to somebody and bring them your dove with your sin all over it, there is going to be blood.

Do not expect to pour out your guts, tell your sin, and then think that they will say, "That is nice. You just need to love yourself. If you could just love yourself everything would be ok."

No, he is not a psychologist. He is a pastor. He is going to correct, and he needs to correct. He will say, "This is what the book of the Law says. The Word of God says that this is bitterness."

"Yes, but do you know what he did to me?"

"Yes, I do. Now, let's deal with your bitterness because that bitterness is hindering and blocking you. Do you not understand that this very thing is destroying your relationships?"

He is not afraid to get into your personal space and say things that no one else has had the courage to say. As mad as you may get when he says these things, you are such a sucker that you go back again.

Why do you go back again? You stomped off telling him that you did not like what you heard. You spat and spewed, and told him that he had a spirit of control and that he did not understand.

You stomped away like a five-year-old that cannot have chocolate saying, "Mom was mean to me."

However, the next day you say, "I just wanted to call you."

Why do you go back?

You keep going back to this person because as much as they got into your personal space and told you the truth, there is something about them that when you are with them, you feel like you belong and you feel safe.

We really need to have more pastors in the church. That way, we would have more places to belong, more temples, houses and homes where people could go and let that baggage go, and let that junk come out.

Not a Pretty Affair

It is not going to be pretty. I do not think the pastor's job is pretty at all. It is quite thankless sometimes. Can you imagine what a priest looked like at the end of the day?

I can imagine him coming home after he has had a rough day. He would have heard things that people should not hear, saw things that people should not see, and he is tired.

He gets to the opening of his tent and his wife says, "Don't you dare come in here with those clothes on. I could smell you from down the road. Go wash and then you can come to dinner."

He would have been covered in blood and guts. Have you ever smelled an animal when it is alive... never mind when it is dead? That is sometimes how it feels to be a pastor. You feel like everybody just splattered all their intestines all over you.

They go home feeling all good and dandy and you feel yucky. You think, "I have to go home and wash off."

That is why this is a ministry people. No one in their right mind does this for fun. It is a calling.

Gets into the "Blood and Guts" of Things

If he is a real pastor, he is going to get personal. He is going to get into the blood and guts of things. He needs to do that in order to help you to be set free.

He is the shepherd that is going to take the staff and the club and he will be there to walk with you through the valley of the shadow of death. However, if you take a wrong step, you are going to get a whack on the head.

That is his job. Paul says that they watch over your souls. You do not realize the responsibility that a pastor has.

For those that are in ministry, you know what I am talking about when there are people under you. You have to take care of them and make sure that they go the right way. When they go the wrong way, you take it personally.

You feel that you failed. It is so personal. You are responsible. You go before God and say, "God, where did I miss it?"

So, when the pastor seems to be being mean and giving you a whack on the knuckles saying, "Wrong move," it is not always because they are trying to be controlling, but because they are watching over your soul.

They are getting personal and getting into your space. Thank God for pastors who have the courage to get into our personal space.

We need more people who will talk less behind the pulpit, but will come and stare us in the face and say, "I see that you and your wife are having problems. You need help."

We need people who will get involved in people's lives. We need somebody who will punch past the social boundary of niceties.

It is no good having everyone be "nice" with a big, veneered smile saying, "How did you find everything today? Lovely!"

Asking the Unasked Questions

The pastor punches past that. He is not very politically correct because he needs to get into your life. As much as it is a bit uncomfortable, we really like it.

"I heard that your husband died. How do you feel about that?"

"I heard that you were raped by your father at a very young age. Let's talk about that."

"I heard that you had a homosexual lifestyle. Come and tell me about that. I want to hear the details."

These are questions that a pastor will ask. When it comes to things that are especially hurtful, you would think that people do not want to talk about them - but you are so wrong.

You have no idea how much we all need to talk about those things.

"Are you still having a problem with pornography? Let's go and talk about it over dinner."

That is a pastor. That is who he is, and he senses that thing in you. He is prepared to go the distance, if you are prepared to offer that sin up in order to break free. He will be there if you are prepared to let him go with you through the valley of the shadow of death, and you do not fear that evil.

That rod and staff are there for you to help you through the process. This is what we need in the church. Do you prophets understand this?

Hey Prophets! Do not be surprised if God has called you to take a leadership position and this is where he takes you first. You need this. Before you can bring out the chisel and say, "Die already" I hope that you know how to set God's people free.

I hope that you know how to bring them deliverance and give them a place to belong. I hope that you lead them through the valley and into the light before you are ready to anoint them, appoint them, and make them be who you think they need to be.

They need to go through a process first, and it is indeed the pastor who takes them through that process.

5. Core Desire: To help others

The pastor also has a core desire to help others. Sit in a room with people and ask them what really burns in them for ministry.

You will have the prophets saying, "I want to heal the broken-hearted and I want to see everybody fulfilling their place."

The evangelists will say, "I just want people to have Jesus." They will bring the fire and talk about demons.

Then, you have the pastor who says,

"I am just happy to help people. I would like to be there to see people rise up. I would like to take them through and see them be what God has called them to be.

I do not always have the answers of what God has called them to do, but I just want to see them happy and flourishing. I am tired of seeing believers backsliding and not caring. I want to see them successful in their marriage and being good Christians."

That may sound boring to some, but it is the core desire of a pastor. He wants to see the best come out of each one. That may sound boring to some, but having someone like that in your life means everything.

They will say, "I do not care about your past, your anointing, your ministry, or what you have to bring me. I just want to see you flourish. I want you to come to the place where you are where God wants you to be.

"Whether that is being a vessel of gold or clay, honor or dishonor, I do not care. I love you the same. I just want you to flourish and shine with what you have."

We need more of that in our lives. Indeed, the pastor is one with the ultimate other-orientation.

6. Takes Care of the Church! (Takes Care of the Temple)

The pastor takes care of the temple. In John 2, Jesus decided to braid a whip and whip the moneychangers. He had himself a party. He was livid!

> **John 2:17** Then His disciples remembered that it was written, "Zeal for Your house has eaten Me up."

I never quite understood that, but as I came to look at the pastor, it made perfect sense. Do you know the guy that always wants that church building? How many have preached that this is status quo garbage?

I preached that too, but it turns out that it is one of the signs of the pastor. Who knew? Jesus was zealous and jealous over the house of God. Guess who took care of the tabernacle in the Old Testament?

The priests were the ones that took care. They are the ones that carried the ark as well. Even in the wilderness, when they had to go to one place and then the other, it was the priests that took everything down, made sure it was folded properly and put away.

The rules were very strict. Only the priests took care of the tabernacle and no one else was allowed to touch it. In fact, David messed that up. He just put the tabernacle on a cart and as a result God slayed some poor guy there that was trying to help out.

Why did that happen? It was because it was the priests that were meant to take care of the tabernacle personally and God was making a point.

"I want my priests taking care of this. Do not come with some new thing that you think is a cooler way to take care of my church. Do not bring the world in and build my church. Do not bring the world in and set a structure in a gathering. This is for my priests to do."

Fusses Over the Building

They are the ones that are zealous about creating an environment. They are the ones making sure that there is a mothers' room in the church because they know that the mothers have children, but they still want to listen to the message.

So, they suggest having a mothers' room with a TV, so that the mothers can still be a part of the service. Only pastors think of that. You and I do not care. We just say, "More Lord. Glory Lord, glory!"

The poor mothers with the babies do not have anyone thinking about them. Well, the pastor is thinking about those mothers. The pastor is also thinking about the guy that has to check the cars outside.

He is thinking about how comfy the seats are. He is thinking how those old, wooden pews have to go because people are falling asleep in them. He is saying, "Let's get something better and brighter. When people come in here, they must feel the presence of God.

"They must feel like they belong. They must feel good about this hub that I am creating, because I am creating an environment."

When you see someone who is carrying on like that, you are looking at someone who is indeed a pastor. That is a part of their calling. However, that is not the only sign. If that is all they care about, that does not mean that they are a pastor.

Remember that we are looking at all the signs here. Do not just look at one and say, "That is me. So then, I must be a pastor." There are a few signs and you should be able to relate to many more than just one.

7. Does Not "Let Go" of People Easily

Here is a big problem for a pastor. He does not let go very easily. This is one that I have lived one hundred times for myself. Have you ever seen those people that just do not let go?

You left their church and they are still phoning and nagging and nagging. You think, "Let me go."

They are pastors. Would a shepherd just let a sheep roll down a hill and say, "Shame… there goes fluffy… sorry about that. I guess he is going to miss the nine o'clock meeting?"

That is not the shepherd. The shepherd goes after the one sheep that is rolling down the hill and makes the whole congregation wait as he takes care of that one that needs help. He battles to let go.

That is the best thing about the pastor and the worst thing about the pastor. As a pastor, it is the one thing that I love because it connects me to those that God has given me. I feel the spiritual connection, and when they leave, I travail.

I remember going to the Lord with this. I said, "Lord, there is something wrong with me. No one else seems to have a problem letting go."

When someone left, I would travail, cry, and pray for them for a year or two down the line. I was wondering what was wrong with me - why I could not let go, and why it hurt so much.

I went to the Lord and told him to take it away. I said, "I am done with all this feeling. I am done with all this travailing over that one sheep."

The Lord said, "It is meant to hurt. If it did not hurt, you never loved them. It is meant to be hard to let go. Otherwise, they were never connected in the first place. It is a ministry."

If you are the kind of person that no matter what people have done to you, you battle to let them go, know that it is such a clear sign of one that is called to be a pastor.

8. Protective Over the Flock

Now, the prophets do not like this next sign. The pastor is protective over the flock. He is like David taking out those wolves, the bear, and the lion. If you really want to upset a pastor and see him hop and skip in the pulpit, mess with his flock.

If you come in with your heretical doctrine, holding a bible study on Wednesday night teaching something different than what he is teaching, then watch him spit and spew.

You say, "He is just not feeling the spirit."

That is possible, but could it also be that he knows his flock, their needs, and where they are at spiritually, and he knows exactly what is going on behind the scenes? Could it be that this is why he does not want you saying what you are saying?

If he is a true pastor, he has gotten in their faces. He knows what is going on in their personal lives. He knows things that you do not know. He knows that if you are equipping them with something that they are not ready to take on yet, you are doing more harm than good.

If you are a prophet, you may just jump in there saying, "This is the place where you belong. You need more anointing, you need more fire, and you need to go out."

Seeing Things From a Fresh Perspective

Yes, you are absolutely right. However, are they ready? Are they ready for that anointing? Are they ready for the word that you know is from God?

I do not doubt that what you are sharing is from God, but are they ready for it? Just because you felt something in the spirit does not mean that you need to open your mouth and speak it.

I have written a whole school on the prophetic, and there, I teach that just because God speaks does not mean that you have to jump up and speak now.

That pastor has been travailing with them every day and he knows that they are getting to that place where they are getting ready to shine. However, if they run too quickly, they are going to trip and fall and that could ruin them.

That means that they may never come back and feel comfortable enough to belong. So yes, he gets mad. Sometimes he even looks a bit controlling.

He says, "You are not allowed to have that meeting. You cannot go and minister to my flock."

Sometimes they are just plain controlling and I am so not going to let them get away with that. Yet, if he is a real pastor, he has an instinct.

Listen, don't you dare mess with one of my team. If you mess with one of my spiritual family, I will come down on you so hard and I do not even care if you think that you are justified. They are my kids. Do not mess with my kids.

Most of you have children of your own. Let's say that someone comes into your home and tells your child, "I think that you should become this, you should go there, and you should eat that."

You would say, "Who do you think you are?"

If they said something bad to your child, you would say, "Get out of my house! Go teach your own children. These are my kids."

That is how a pastor feels over his flock. Those are his children and his sheep. Do not push them somewhere that they do not need to go. That is a sign of a pastoral call. That is why we need each other.

The Pastoral Failure – Working Solo

The failure that I see in the pastor is not that he is overprotective. There is nothing wrong with that. The failure is that they do not work with the rest of the fivefold ministry.

If they did, they would have the input of the prophet, the pattern of the apostle, and the all the fire that is needed from the evangelist, to deal with the things that need to be dealt with.

However, he ends up trying to be everything, falls short, and then realizes that he is losing a grip on the sheep, and becomes controlling. His failure is not the fire to be protective.

His fault is that he tries to work alone. However, I do not think that this is just the fault of the pastor. A few of the other ministries have the same problem.

9. The "Jack-of-all-Trades" Anointing

The pastor is a jack-of-all-trades. That can sometimes be frustrating for a pastor. He is the jack-of-all-trades, master-of-none. He can pray a bit for healing, he can give a prophetic word every now and again, and he can be a teacher.

Someone may ask, "What is your calling?"

You feel in yourself that you are not really one thing. You feel that you are a bit of everything. You think, "I can prophesy, I can see visions, I get words of knowledge, I get words of wisdom, I have flowed in the external anointing, and I have seen people slain in the spirit.

Yet, on the other hand, I can counsel people and I have seen Jesus really move and minister to people's needs. So, which one of the fivefold ministry am I?"

You are all of them.

It makes sense. I am a mom, so sometimes I have to be a nurse, sometimes I have to be the dishwasher, and sometimes I am the bed maker. I even need to be there to teach them to brush their teeth.

I am a little bit of everything. You need to be whatever you need to be for your kids, right? It is the same for the pastor. He has to meet the needs of the people. So, he has to become all things to all men.

He has to be a jack-of-all-trades. Whatever anointing is needed at that time, he has to be able to get it. That is why it seems that they never go to one big office. He never moves in one big sign or wonder, or one big anointing.

It seems that he hops here and there, and it can be confusing, especially if you are the one that is called to be a pastor.

You may think, "What is wrong with me? What am I, Lord? I thought I was a prophet, but now I am sharing an evangelistic message. Then suddenly, you have me teaching on marriage and doing something else. What is up with that?"

You are a pastor. God will pick you up and use you to meet the need that is there in the people. The message you preach will depend on the condition of your flock. You will be there to meet them where they are at.

It can be a bit confusing sometimes, but when you find your place, you see that it is normal and that it does not depend on you.

I have had pastors who were pastor-teachers their whole lives but then one day someone comes in sick, and they move miraculously in signs and wonders just that once.

You say, "Am I an evangelist now?

No, you are a pastor. That person needed that and so God gave you what you needed. The job is done now. It is actually quite fun. It is a very diverse ministry.

10. Ministry to the Church

Lastly, the pastor's ministry is to the church. He is a shepherd to God's flock. You are not going to see pastors going and pastoring unbelievers. He creates an environment for the church. He is jealous over God's people.

The Ruler that Serves

I have labeled the pastor as the ruler who serves, which seems a little contradictory, but there is no better way to describe him. He is an example and a model. He leads, but he has an anointing to serve and to minister to God's people.

> *Hebrews 13:17 Obey those who rule over you, and be submissive, for they watch out for your souls, as those who must give account. Let them do so with joy and not with grief, for that would be unprofitable for you.*

That is the responsibility of the pastor. He has to give an account to God for the spiritual condition of your soul.

If I walk into a church and I want to see what kind of pastor is in that church, I talk to the congregation.

Paul said, "I see you have this much faith and this much love, but let's work on the hope." He also said, "I see you have a lot of faith, but no love. Let's work on that." (Rom 1:8, Eph 1:15, Col 1:4-5, 1 Thess 1:3)

The condition of the flock will depend on their pastor. The pastor will be called to give an account before God for that. That is a heavy responsibility. Sometimes we overlook that responsibility.

We get all hung up with the abuse that we have seen, and the wrong things that we have seen in the church, but let us allow the pastor to create an environment and give us a place to belong. If you are called to be a pastor, there is so much more that you should be doing.

It is not about standing behind the pulpit. That is the easy part. That is the once a week part. It is like being a mother. When are you a mother? It is at two o'clock in the morning when you have not had much sleep and you have to be up early but your child needs you. That is when you are being a mother.

Are you being a mother on Mother's Day when they bring you roses and tell you how wonderful you are? No. That is the least of it. You are being a mother when they are throwing up because they are sick and you have to clean the floor for the tenth time.

That is being a mother, and that is what it is like to be a pastor too. You are not a pastor when you stand behind the pulpit. You are a pastor when you are getting involved in people's lives and are changing them.

It takes an anointing and a calling to do that. You do not have to stand behind a pulpit to flow in a pastoral ministry. You can do it right where you are, right now with those that God is bringing you.

Regardless of what you think your ministry call is, all of us need this before we can take the Church to the next level. Do not go dumping anointings and callings on people if you have not walked through the valley with them first.

Stand in boldness in the position that has been delegated to you. Stand in humility in the anointing the Holy Spirit has imparted to you. Bring together the best of both worlds, and become instrumental in transforming the Church.

Pastor – the body of Christ is waiting for you. It is waiting for your healing touch. It is waiting for your bold leadership and your willing heart. You have a seed within you that has the potential to produce fruit as we have never seen. Yes, it is a price to pay.

Yes, it is a calling and not just a job description. When James made himself accountable for that calling, the church at Jerusalem set the pace for entire Christendom! How much can the Lord do with the seed in your heart? Well, why not plant it and find out?

THE PASTOR'S PURPOSE

Chapter 07 – The Pastor's Purpose

Jeremiah 23:3-4

> *"But I will gather the remnant of My flock out of all countries where I have driven them, and bring them back to their folds; and they shall be fruitful and increase. 4 I will set up shepherds over them who will feed them; and they shall fear no more, nor be dismayed, nor shall they be lacking," says the Lord.*

Just as the Lord in these end times has raised up the apostles and the prophets, so is He raising up the pastors of a new generation and a new breed. He is raising a shepherd that will stand up and be pastor over the flock that He is gathering to His Body at this time.

Mass Influx of New Believers

Word after word is being spoken right now through the prophets, that there is coming a tremendous increase in harvest - that a mass of souls is coming to the body of Christ. We are told of mass evangelism and a huge influx of unbelievers into the Body of Christ to make up the Bride.

Even now, the Lord is working on the evangelists to bring in the lost, and raising up true evangelists to go into all the nations and gather His people to Him from every tribe and tongue.

His work does not end there! He is also preparing and raising up pastors who will shepherd these new believers who are being brought into the body of Christ.

Anyone Wanting Babies?

You see, it is not good enough to just give birth to hundreds, thousands, and millions of babies. We need somebody to look after these babies after they have come into the Kingdom of God.

You don't just have a baby and expect it to look after itself. There is a lot of responsibility involved and there is a lot that you need to do. There is milk that needs to be fed to these babies. There are diapers that need to be changed. Each baby needs to be held and cared for.

Now who is going to accomplish this massive task of being a parent and a mother to all these hundreds of nations that are coming to the Lord? The evangelist can't do it. He is too busy birthing. He is too busy in travail bringing in the unbelievers.

Enter: Today's Pastors

This is where the pastor steps in. This is where you, as a pastor, are going to play your part in the End Times Church. It involves taking care of those that have come to Christ and those that already belong to Christ.

It involves raising them into spiritual adults, who are mature in the knowledge of the Lord, strong in conviction, and who walk in the power of the Holy Spirit.

Now this is no easy task, and as a pastor you have a tremendous task and responsibility ahead of you. But I want you to know right now that your call to be a pastor was not a coincidence.

It was not by chance that you stand where you do today. Just as each of the other ministries has been trained in their time and in their way, the Lord has been hovering over you and had His hand on you. Your whole life has been to prepare you for this time, and for this work right now in the body of Christ.

Preparation for Growth and Expansion

Time is short, and perhaps the labor pains in your own life have been very rapid and you have been facing a lot of difficulty. You have been facing one trial after another. If this has been happening, it is good news! This is good news, because it means that the Lord is preparing you. He is making you ready and preparing you for growth and expansion, for blessing and an expansion of your ministry.

You are not going to stay where you have been all your life. Perhaps all you have ever managed is to run a congregation of twenty people. Perhaps all you have is a little home cell group. Or maybe you have been a pastor to thousands.

Wherever you are right now, the Lord wants to take you beyond that. He wants to take you further. If you find that your pastorate has been one of struggle and difficulty, don't be discouraged. Through this trial and through this travail there will come a tremendous birth, and tremendous growth and expansion. You will also be rewarded for these times of pushing through. You will be rewarded even in the most adverse of circumstances.

Hold onto that promise, because this is your inheritance and your portion right now. You need to become the good shepherd. You need to become the image of Christ to His people.

The Shepherd Who Succeeds

Let's have a look at the good shepherd. Let's see how he does it. I found so many Scriptures on being a shepherd in the Word, that I had to try and cut a few of them, because there were just so many. I just picked my favorites, but there is so much that the Lord has to speak to you about. Can you see how important the role of a shepherd is?

When we speak about prophets, there is a limited amount in the Old and New Testaments, even though you have the great examples. The Lord never really gave the prophets a specific direction though on how to live their lives and how to treat people.

However, if you look up shepherds and pastors in the Word, you see how much direction the Lord gives and how much importance He lays on the shepherds, because it is a daily task of working through, working things out and raising the people up.

It is just like it is being a mother, taking care of the needs daily. Before you know it, you look back, and your baby is a toddler, a child, an adolescent and then an adult. You are going to take them to that stage, and this is how you will do it.

The Shepherd Leads

Firstly, the shepherd leads. Numbers 27:16-17 says:

> *Let the Lord, the God of the spirits of all flesh, set a man over the congregation,*
> *17 who may go out before them and go in before them, who may lead them out and bring them in, that the congregation of the Lord may not be like sheep which have no shepherd.*

Moses prayed to the Lord and said, "Don't leave your people without a shepherd. Give them somebody strong."

The Lord gave them Joshua to be a shepherd over Israel. Joshua is a strong, positive picture. He doesn't look like a pathetic little nobody that just stood up on Sundays to give a short message does he? Joshua was a warrior who went ahead of the people. He had their backing. He was with them. The people were with him, his heart was knitted to theirs, and they were one body.

You look at poor Moses who was also a tremendous shepherd. He really gave his heart and life for his people, but the people and him were not one. Moses was always getting direction from the Lord, and he laid the foundation. He laid it really well, but the people were always off doing their own thing.

Poor Moses - I bet he was as white as snow from all the gray hair they gave him. He was always struggling and fighting with them. There was Korah, and the Lord had to go and swallow them up with an earthquake. Then there was a rebellion about lack of water, and Moses had to strike the rock.

Another time the Lord wanted to wipe the Israelites out because they were worshiping the foreign gods and Moses had to say, "No Lord, don't kill them."

Then he had to go back and say, "You naughty people! I told you not to do that!"

It just looked like one struggle after the next. It was not so with Joshua however. The people's hearts were knitted to Joshua. He and they were of one mind and one spirit.

We are known as a body, but when I look at Moses, it sometimes felt like he was a bit disconnected. A head without a body to follow!

Thank the Lord for the seventy elders and Joshua by his side to hold him up.

Half the time he was a head bouncing around until the Lord said, "Hey, you need some help here."

Then He gave Moses a couple of arms and legs. After that, he did so much more.

Joshua though, had a people who were with him. They were his body, and they conquered Canaan's land. They took the land for the people of Israel and they went in and accomplished, in a very short space of time, what Moses and the whole nation of Israel could not accomplish in over forty years!

A United Body is Powerful

Why could Moses not accomplish that in all that time? He was with them for nearly fifty years! It was because they were not of one mind and one spirit. The body was going in one direction and the head was going in another.

You look at Joshua though. What do you see? You see a body that was knitted with the head and whose borders were extended. The nations trembled in front of them. The nations were scattered and they took the land. There was victory after victory and the power of God was with them.

The nations trembled and the world looked on and said, "The nation of Israel - their God is a mighty God."

Now that is what is going to be said of you as you bring your body together, and as the Lord places you as head over that body to represent Him. Are you getting the picture of a warrior, and of the man or woman of God that Christ has called the pastor to be?

Can you see how much you can accomplish by being a shepherd who leads -by being a shepherd who is strong and brings his flock together? You get revelation, you go ahead of your sheep, and you are a true leader that people want to look up to and follow.

Their hearts are knitted to you and your heart is knitted to them. You are one. You are bonded with cords that cannot be broken. As you are one you are going out there and you are changing this world. Action is coming, and so is change. There is daily growth taking place.

It looks a little different to how things have looked in the past doesn't it? If you can see Joshua and the nation of Israel standing with him, that is what the Lord wants for you and your congregation.

He wants you to go out there and take the land, not as one leader running ahead of the pack. You need to go out as a body, as a unit going out into this world and taking the land for Christ. You have a mission as a body, not just as a pastor. A head cannot have a mission without a body. Your congregation is your body.

He is Gentle

The shepherd who succeeds is gentle. Isaiah 40:11 says:

> *He will feed His flock like a shepherd; He will gather the lambs with His arm, and carry them in His bosom, and gently lead those who are with young.*

I just love this image of the shepherd, of taking the little lambs in his arms and holding them to his bosom, of leading gently those that are with young. Can you see the gentleness and the consideration?

You know, sometimes as a leader we expect those who follow us to be as mature as we are and to have the same vision and initiative. We don't realize that they are young, that they are with young, and they do not have the initiative.

They do not have the vision. They do not have the same fire burning in them as what burns in you. You know, it just takes a bit of consideration to pick up that little lamb and hold it to your bosom. Sometimes that is all that you need to do to give somebody a bit of what you have.

Instead of trying to hammer them and saying, "What's wrong with you people? You sit here every Sunday and you are not going out and doing anything. Don't you understand that the Lord has given us this vision? Don't you understand that the Lord wants us to expand? Don't you realize that this is what we have to do?"

Sometimes all the shepherd needs to do is bend down, pick up the lamb, hold it against his bosom and say, "It's okay. I'm here for you. I love you. It's all right. You don't need to be a sheep. It's okay to just be a little lamb for now."

You Impart Through Love

You would be surprised that when you take that attitude, how quickly growth will take place in your congregation. You will see how quickly they will start getting your vision. If you cannot impart it to them through the words of your mouth, then you need to impart it to them through your actions.

You need to give them the vision in your heart through the way you speak to them personally. You need to extend your hand a little bit and get in there. Speak to them about their lives and their problems, and about what is going on with them.

As you are sharing with them openly, even if you are talking about them, they are going to pick up your spirit and what is in you. You don't need to take the vision that the Lord has given you and force it down their throats. If they would just open their heart to you, you could impart it through your bosom.

That is what you need to be doing - just taking the time to come off your pulpit a little bit and spend some time with those lambs. It doesn't even matter what you are talking about. Just get them to open their hearts to you. By them doing this, that anointing that is in you and that vision that is burning in you, will automatically be imparted to them, because their hearts are open wide to receive. They will drink in everything you have to give them, but you have to get them to open their hearts first.

That is why you need to be gentle. Some people do not respond to a chisel. Some people need a bit of coaxing, a bit of gentleness, and tender loving care to open their hearts. If you do that, you will win them, and once you have won them, they are with you right until the end.

He Prepares Their Hearts

The shepherd who succeeds lays a foundation. Isaiah 44:28 says:

> *Who says of Cyrus, 'He is My shepherd, And he shall perform all My pleasure, Saying to Jerusalem, "You shall be built,"And to the temple, "Your foundation shall be laid."*

It is vital that you lay the foundation in the hearts of God's people. What does that mean? It means that you are daily and weekly preparing their hearts for what is to come in the body of Christ. You are preparing and building into them a foundation on which the prophets and apostles can lay the structure that is to come. You see, the prophets and apostles cannot put up the structure if the hearts of God's people are not ready to receive it.

You are saying right now, "Lord, I want revival. Lord, bring your fire. Bring your glory. Bring the rain. Bring everything, Lord. I will even accept snow if it is going to bring change!"

But you know, it is simply not going to come that way, because the hearts of God's people are not ready to receive it. Until their hearts are ready, the anointing will not come.

Putting the Pieces Together

When did the power of God come down on Solomon's temple? It came down when it was built and was ready to receive the anointing. You have corpses sitting in your pews. That doesn't look like Solomon's temple. No anointing is going to come gushing out of nowhere to land on them, because their hearts are not ready for it.

You need to build them up. Their hearts must be prepared. As their hearts are prepared, the power is going to come. You are going to get the rain, the snow, the fire, and anything else you want, but their hearts must be prepared. It is your responsibility to prepare their hearts for the revival.

It is not enough to ask the Lord for the end result. It is not enough to say, "Lord if only we had revival, man this church would grow. Lord, if only we had the power gifts to manifest. Oh Lord, I'd just lay hands on these people, they would fall under the power and the glory would come. Then we would just grow and I wouldn't need to worry about finances ever again. I would just be invited to preach everywhere."

Preparing the Soil for Revival

It is not going to happen, because the hearts of God's people are not ready for it. The anointing is not coming for your good pleasure. It is coming for theirs. The gifts work that way. The Lord is not going to give you the anointing just because it is fun for you. The Lord is going to give you the anointing because the people desire it and suck it out of you.

The more people you have in the congregation saying, "Lord give our pastor the anointing, because we want it," the greater chance you have of it coming. They are going to draw it out of you. The Lord is not going to give you anything they are not asking for, so you need to be careful what your congregation is asking for.

You had better pray that they are not asking, "Oh Lord, give us another pastor. This one's killing us every Sunday with his sermons!"

What are your congregation asking for? Whatever they are praying for is what the Lord is going to grant them through you. So if you are wanting revival power, if you are wanting change, it begins with them. Their hearts have to be ready for it. They have to be desiring it. The fire has to be burning in them.

You have to lay a foundation, and as you lay that foundation, it will be like seeds sprouting. The seed has always been there since the day they were saved. You just need to water it. You just need to give it some food.

As their hearts change they will, on their own, spontaneously start crying out to God and saying, "God give us revival. Father we need your touch."

As they do that He is going to come on you as their leader and as their head, to give them what they are crying out for.

Just as a parent would give a child the food that they crave and the desire of their hearts, so will the Lord give you not the desires of your heart, but their desires. That is what the gifts are for. They are for flowing out, not taking in. Get their hearts ready, and the anointing will come on you. Get the foundation in them and you have the power. That is the way it works.

Gather the Flock

You must gather the flock together. I have already covered this, but Jeremiah 31:10 says:

> *Hear the word of the Lord, O nations, and declare it in the isles afar off, and say, 'He who scattered Israel will gather him, and keep him as a shepherd does his flock.'*

Keep your flock together. Have one purpose and one vision. If you can just get two believers in one heart and in one spirit to pray for revival, it will come. Well how many people do you have in your gathering or in your congregation?

If you could get all their hearts in the same direction with the same passion and all praying for revival, you are in for a flood that will come upon you as a tidal wave! Bring them together, give them a singleness of purpose, and get them excited about it. Give them a goal and make them feel a part of it, and the blessing will come on you to give to them.

He Protects from Deception

The good shepherd protects the flock against deception. You guard them against the wolf. You are vigilant, not because you are afraid that somebody else is going to steal your sheep. You truly care about the flock. When a wolf comes and starts nibbling on their heels, you are going to beat that wolf with a stick!

You say, "How dare you touch my sheep! That's mine. Don't touch my sheep!"

That is the true good shepherd. He is honestly caring. You know, heaven help any mean little kid that comes up and slaps one of my children. I am there and I want to give him a piece of my mind - and maybe a piece of some of my fist too. It is my child you are touching.

"Don't you dare touch my daughter! Who do you think you are?"

That is how you should be with your sheep when it comes to deception and the wolf.

You should not be saying, "Well if they believe him you know I'm going to lose my pedestal here. Nobody is going to come to church on Sunday."

No, that is not the motivation. You are not there for the sheep to meet your need. Immediately what rises up from within the pit of your stomach is, "How dare you touch God's anointed!"

You are there to protect them in a flash. You are there to snatch them out of the mouths of the lion and the wolf. That is what the good shepherd does. That is his heart, and that is his attitude.

He Feeds the Sheep

The good shepherd feeds the sheep. Mark 6:34 says:

> *And Jesus, when He came out, saw a great multitude and was moved with compassion for them, because they were like sheep not having a shepherd. So He began to teach them many things.*

The Lord didn't say, "Man these sheep look lost! Oh well guys, let's go home. Dinner's waiting."

No. It says He saw them, His heart was moved, and then He taught them. It wasn't enough just to see them scattered. He pulled them together and poured into them. He gave them some spiritual food that built them up.

Your sheep need to be fed daily. They need to be given the meat of the Word and the water of the Spirit. They need to be fed wine - the glory hallelujah anointing - but they also need to be fed bread.

You need to say, "These are the principles of the Word. Eat and be filled."

How else does a child grow if you are not feeding them bread and water? They won't grow on air. You cannot just expect the sheep to take care of themselves and say, "Oh well, grow now. There you go, sheep. Grow up."

You have to feed them something. Not even a plant can survive without sunlight and water. We have learned that one. If you don't water your plants for a while they die. Do you think your sheep are any different? You need to feed them all the time.

You don't just skip meals. You don't think, "Oh well you know what? I'm just too tired. I couldn't be cared to get into the anointing to give these sheep anything."

You know, when my little baby wakes up for her morning feed I don't turn round and say, "You know what? She can survive without it."

What kind of mother would I be? I would wake up to a baby that was way less weight than what it should be. A couple more attitudes like that and I would have a dead baby on my hands. You don't skip meals! That is not the way it works.

You don't say, "Fend for yourself today. I don't feel like feeding you today."

If you do that you will come back next Sunday and your baby is going to be dead. You can't afford to skip meals here. This isn't a weight loss program. You are trying to raise good, strong healthy children to adulthood. You need to feed them all the time.

Being Transparent

The good shepherd is transparent and open. He shares his heart. People look at him and say, "I want to be like that!"

They are part of him and he is part of them. They are his family - his flesh and blood. It is just like the blood going through your veins into each part of your body. It belongs to you and to the members of your body.

The blood that runs through you runs through your congregation as well. They are you and you are them. You are the one body partaking of the same covenant, and partaking of the same blood of Christ.

You are one. They know you, and you know them. They are an integral part of your personal and social life.

They know your heart, they see your care, and they see you bend down and pick up that lamb. They see you pour your heart out. They see you working hard, and they respect you and love you for it.

Laying Down Your Life

You lay down your life for the sheep. John 10:11 says:

> *I am the good shepherd. The good shepherd gives His life for the sheep.*

I think that this Scripture just really sums up the whole illustration of the good shepherd and the points that I have been going through in this chapter. He lays down His life for the sheep. He lays down His life so that theirs may be raised up. He puts aside His needs so that he can meet theirs. As He puts aside all of those things, so the Body begins to grow.

Do you know what the exciting part is? It is that as that Body begins to grow, the Lord rises up with them. So, you may be putting aside your life. You may be putting aside your desires and your needs and everything else, but as you do so, they are growing, because you are feeding them. As they are growing, you are on the top of the pile and you are growing up with them.

So perhaps it means giving your life. Perhaps it means giving up everything, and it seems like sacrifice after sacrifice. However, the reward and the promise remain. They will rise up because of your self-sacrifice, and the reward and the promise will come upon you.

The Lord will gather a flock. You will be placed over them, and His power will rest upon you. First you need to lay down your life for the sheep though.

Perfection is Overrated

In conclusion I just want to say, the Lord requires your faithfulness, not your perfection. I have gone through many points here, and you are probably thinking, "Oh boy, if that is what a pastor is, there is no way that I can match up to that!"

The Lord requires faithfulness, not perfection. You are going to miss it. You are going to fail Him. You are going to lose a few sheep to the wolves, and pull out an ear or a leg as the Scripture says.

But that is not what the Lord is looking at. He is not looking at your success rate. He is looking at your heart. If the motivation of your heart is true, the fruit will come in its season, and it will be big, strong, and juicy. It is what is inside that counts. It is your attitude.

You see, the Lord can make you into the good shepherd. He can take the image you are, the mess of the image that you are right now, and He can shape you into the image of Christ who is the good shepherd. It is not what you do, it is not what you say or how hard you try. It is the attitude of your heart.

If you will just submit to Christ and give Him what you are and what you have, He can make you into that shepherd.

Your Training Starts Here – The Secret

At the end of the day, it is the Lord Jesus that called you so He is also the one that will enable you for this task. The Church is hungry and looking for leaders that will take up the 2am feeding time.

They are seeking leaders that they can follow and feel secure around. As the Lord raises you up for ministry, realize that if you have been called to be a teacher, prophet or apostle… your training starts right here!

Paul tells Timothy that an elder must be able to rule his house well if he is to be trusted with the house of God. How much more for you if you feel God leading you further in a fivefold ministry call?

Do not think that you can skip this step. I think that especially the prophets wish that they could jump past the role of "pastor" but I have some news for you! If you want to excel in any of the others, you need the training and diligence that being a pastor gives you.

Sure enough, you might not remain in this office. The Lord might do with you like He did with Peter and Barnabus and send them out. However, they all started somewhere. Peter took care, as an elder, of the church in Jerusalem.

Could it be that the Lord is challenging you right now to become a good shepherd before you become a mighty warrior? May you discover this secret – that this is the hidden treasure of your call. This is the missing piece you have been looking for.

The call to being a leader is one of servanthood. It is one of doing the work of the ministry as God requires it of you. Take your time to develop your call. Take time to become the good Shepherd. You might find yourself like Moses and David were found by the Holy Spirit.

Alone, in the wilderness taking care of the few sheep, only to be given a much larger flock to care for. Be diligent with your sheep now, and watch how the Lord opens your way to become his end times leader, set to change hearts and lives.

About the Author

Born in Bulawayo, Zimbabwe and raised in South Africa, Colette had a zeal to serve the Lord from a young age. Coming from a long line of Christian leaders and having grown up as a pastor's kid she is no stranger to the realities of ministry. Despite having to endure many hardships such as her parent's divorce, rejection, and poverty, she continues to follow after the Lord passionately. Overcoming these obstacles early in her life has built a foundation of compassion and desire to help others gain victory in their lives.

Since then, the Lord has led Colette, with her husband Craig Toach, to establish *Apostolic Movement International,* a ministry to train and minister to Christian leaders all over the world, where they share all the wisdom that the Lord has given them through each and every time they chose to walk through the refining fire in their personal lives, as well as in ministry.

In addition, Colette is a fantastic cook, an amazing mom to not only her 4 natural children, but to her numerous spiritual children all over the world. Colette is also a renowned author, mentor, trainer and a woman that has great taste in shoes! The scripture to "be all things to all men" definitely applies here, and the Lord keeps adding to that list of things each and every day.

How does she do it all? Experience through every book and teaching the life of an apostle firsthand, and get the insight into how the call of God can make every aspect of your life an incredible adventure.

Read more at www.colette-toach.com

Connect with Colette Toach on Facebook!
www.facebook.com/ColetteToach

Check Colette out on Amazon.com at:
www.amazon.com/author/colettetoach

Recommendations by the Author

Note: All reference of AMI refers to Apostolic Movement International.

If you enjoyed this book, I know you will also love the following books and recommendations.

The Fivefold Offices for Today

Book 1 of the Fivefold Office Series

By Colette Toach

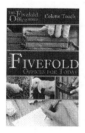

The fivefold ministry has been a mystery that is only being resurrected in the Church today.

You see people rising up with the different callings, you see how God brings these different individuals together, and calls them to set the Church afire, but what are the fivefold offices exactly, and where do you fit in?

Are you an Apostle, Prophet, Teacher, Pastor, or Evangelist? Are you called to walk the social, business, or ministry road? It is time to reveal the road ahead of you, and to rise up into the fullness of your call.

Where you are now is great, but God has so much more in store for you than you realize. It is time to take hold of the reality of your call to the fivefold offices.

Today's Evangelist

Book 2 of the Fivefold Office Series

By Colette Toach

As an evangelist, you are called to start churches, to bring life to the dead, to bring people into the embrace of the Holy Spirit, and open their eyes to the power of Christ.

In this book, Colette will show you where the evangelist came from, what their role is in the fivefold ministry, and how and where they operate. So be prepared to go higher and understand your call as an evangelist like never before.

The Minister's Handbook

By Colette Toach

This is your manual on effective ministry. Whether you are dealing with an unexpected demon manifestation or you need to give marital counsel, you will find the answers here.

Colette Toach gives it to you in plain language. She gives you the steps 1, 2, 3 of how to do what God has called you to do. Keep a copy on hand, because you will come back to it time and time again!

How to Get People to Follow You

By Colette Toach

Colette pours out leadership secrets straight from the Throne Room that will make you the kind of leader others want to follow. No more hitting your head on the wall. No more being the only one excited about your vision.

Sharing from her own failures and triumphs, Colette hands you the keys to your success as a leader.

How to Hear the Voice of God (Study Group Kit)

By Colette Toach

Knowing the Lord is more than just understanding the principles of the Word. It is learning to know when He is speaking and to share in the secrets in His heart.

By the time you are finished with this course, you will discover that God does not have favorites, but that every believer can hear from Him clearly.

If you are ready to experience the reality of the Lord in your life, then dive in!

Fivefold Ministry School

www.fivefold-school.com

You Can Be a Success in Ministry!

My passion is to see you realize yours! I understand the years in the desert. I know what it feels like to have a fire shut up in your bones, knowing that God has something greater for you.

That is why together with my husband Craig Toach, we have trained up our own Fivefold Ministry team and in association with apostles all over the world, we hold in our hands the resources to launch you into your ministry!

Here is What We Offer to Prepare You for Your Fivefold Ministry Calling

- Identify Your Fivefold Ministry Calling
- Disciple and Mentor Relationship
- Ministry Certification, Credentials and Ordination
- Ministry Training Materials That Are Totally Unique
- Fivefold Ministry Training That Affects More Than Your Mind
- Student Only Benefits

Contact Information

To check out our wide selection of materials, go to:
www.ami-bookshop.com

Do you have any questions about any products?

Contact us at: +1 (760) 466 - 7679
(9am to 5pm California Time, Weekdays Only)

E-mail Address: admin@ami-bookshop.com

Postal Address:

> A.M.I.
> 5663 Balboa Ave #416
> San Diego, CA 92111, USA

Facebook Page:
http://www.facebook.com/ApostolicMovementInternational

YouTube Page:
https://www.youtube.com/c/ApostolicMovementInternational

Twitter Page: https://twitter.com/apmoveint

Amazon.com Page: www.amazon.com/author/colettetoach

AMI Bookshop – It's not Just Knowledge, It's **Living Knowledge**